THE
CONSERVATIVE
COMEBACK

THE
CONSERVATIVE
COMEBACK

★ **TODD LONG** ★

CREATION
HOUSE
A STRANG COMPANY

THE CONSERVATIVE COMEBACK by Todd Long
Published by Creation House
A Strang Company
600 Rinehart Road
Lake Mary, Florida 32746
www.strangbookgroup.com

Unless otherwise noted, all Scripture quotations are from the King James Version of the Bible.

Scripture quotations marked NLT are from the Holy Bible, New Living Translation, copyright © 1996. Used by permission of Tyndale House Publishers, Inc., Wheaton, IL 60189. All rights reserved.

Design Director: Bill Johnson
Cover design by Justin Evans

Library of Congress Control Number: 2010920441
International Standard Book Number: 978-1-61638-145-5

10 11 12 13 — 9 8 7 6 5 4 3 2
Printed in the United States of America

DEDICATION

To my children Noah and Natalia, my greatest joys, in the hope that this small book teaches and reminds them of their heritage and instills in them a desire to fight for our Founders' values so they, too, may be a blessing to their fellow Americans.

CONTENTS

ACKNOWLEDGMENTS

I WOULD LIKE TO thank everyone who made this book a reality. Particularly, my dad, Bill Long, who worked so hard to edit, organize my thoughts, and provide critical research that made this book possible. I also want to thank my beautiful wife, Ninette, and good friends Rosa Alvarez, Joyce Bowden, Jim Kohlman, Bill Winsemann, and Simon Conway for their contributions to the editing of the book, as well as my book reviewers whose opinions I value so much.

This book certainly would not be possible without my inspirational radio and TV show hosts, Glenn Beck, Neil Boortz, Rush Limbaugh, Bill O'Reilly, Sean Hannity, and (the man who hates evil more than anyone I know) Dr. Michael Savage. They all have a reverence for our Founders' values and speak the truth from their unique perspectives the best they know how. I have learned so much from each one.

As an adult, my spiritual guidance has largely been the product of three great men and their families: Pastor John Jeyaseelan of Bethel Ministries; Pastor Chris Sarno of International Miracle Center; and Pastor Keith Tower of Highpoint Church. Each brought me closer to Jesus and continually demonstrates to my family and me what it means to be a devoted Christian. Their impact has completely changed my life for the better.

Finally and most importantly, I want to thank God and the precious family He blessed me with: my wife Ninette, my children Noah and Natalia, my dad (Bill), mom (Eileen), and sister (Robin), for their love and support.

INTRODUCTION

R EFLECTING ON HIS past, Mark Twain observed that when he was fifteen, he thought his father was so stupid that he could hardly bear to be in the same room with him. But when he reached twenty-five, he was astounded by how much the old man had learned in ten years.

Just like Twain, as America confronts the daunting challenges of the twenty-first century, we would all do well to take a fresh look at the ideas, values, and principles of our nation's Founding Fathers. This is particularly the case for my Republican Party, bruised and bloody though it be after the elections of 2008, well down in the polls of public opinion, and haunted by mocking Democrats that Republican policies and prescriptions for the nation's needs are out of touch and irrelevant.

Over the last decade, the Republican Party (the historic standard-bearers of our Founders' principles) has lost its way. The party's troubles, "have a lot to do with the fact that Americans didn't stop liking what the Republican party is supposed to deliver—they stopped liking what the GOP actually delivered."[1] Some members are wandering the desert, confused about who they are and what they stand for; others are lured by the call of wealth and power away from doing the people's business; while still others unashamedly trek down whatever path carries them through to the next election. This must end if conservatism is to regain its place of influence in American politics. And most important, it must end if America is to reclaim its position of leadership and respect around the world and our citizens are to enjoy personal freedom, prosperity, and a high quality of life.

In my view, a "Conservative Comeback" is not only essential, but well within our ability to carry out. To paraphrase an old Twain saying, "Rumors of our death are greatly exaggerated."[2]

In the pages that follow, I argue that the Founders—Washington, Jefferson, Adams, Madison, Franklin, and their colleagues—"got it right" from the start in establishing a philosophy and system of government on which the strongest, richest, most welcoming and most envied nation on earth was built. What they bequeathed to us in terms of ideas, beliefs, and values, and in their examples of courageous, inspired leadership provide essential guidance as we try to put America back on the right track.

The Founders believed passionately that individual freedom and rights came from God and not man. They placed special emphasis on respect for the rule of law; a strong military to preserve hard-won freedoms; a small and efficient federal government given specific, limited powers under the Constitution; individualism, hard work, and personal responsibility; and a society based on the traditional family and Judeo-Christian values. These fundamental beliefs and principles—which I consider to be at the heart of conservatism—in my view constitute the unchallengeable bedrock on which a great nation can be built and sustained.

My own views on this subject were shaped in my early years, growing up in a small family with midwestern roots and Christian values. I remember always having a strong sense of national pride and a passion for understanding entrepreneurial opportunity and economics. With a father employed in the State Department, and my family living just outside Washington, D.C. in the seventies and early eighties, it was not unusual that I developed an interest in world and national events.

From the outset, I believed that what made America strong were the values of the people who fought and died to create it during the American Revolution, and which have been passed on to each new generation. What they established was then made better by great leaders like Abraham Lincoln and Dr. Martin Luther King, Jr., who improved our nation by ending slavery and fighting for equal rights and justice for all people. They never changed our Founders' principles; they led courageously to make sure that the principles applied to everyone.

I joined millions of other Americans in the eighties, cheering when President Ronald Reagan prophetically told the world that America, strengthened through its values and free-market system, would defeat communism. I witnessed America's return to prosperity when President Reagan dramatically reduced the tax burden on Americans, giving the people back much of their hard-earned money.

President Reagan simply let freedom and capitalism work, producing wealth and a high standard of living for millions of Americans—and our economy flourished. He understood how priceless and fragile freedom is; how power corrupts; and how government naturally tends to grow out of control and overwhelm the very freedoms our Constitution guarantees:

> In this present crisis, government is not the solution to
> our problems—government is the problem...We are not,
> as some would have us believe, doomed to an inevitable
> decline. So, with all the creative energy at our command,
> let us begin an era of national renewal. Let us renew our
> determination, our courage, and our strength. And let us
> renew our faith and our hope.[3]
>
> —PRESIDENT RONALD REAGAN
> INAUGURAL ADDRESS, JANUARY 20, 1981

In the post-Reagan period, however, the nation—and those who purportedly championed conservative values—began to lose their way. Fiscal responsibility and any acknowledgment of the limitation on the power of the federal government went out the window. Ironically and tragically, the biggest offenders included Republicans, especially from 2001 to 2006, the political party most entrusted to champion conservative values, and particularly limited government and fiscal responsibility.

In 2002, the Republicans passed the nation's largest farm subsidy bill at a cost of tens of billions of dollars annually, with tens of millions going to people who did no farming at all.[4] One year later, Republicans enacted the largest expansion of the welfare state since Lyndon Johnson created Medicare in 1965, with a prescription-drug entitlement that did not include a way to pay for it. At the same time, they spent tens of billions annually on local earmark projects to help secure votes, money, and preserve their own concentrated power. Opportunism was rampant and it seemed clear that the Republican Congress cared far more for themselves and their careers than for being good stewards of our nation.

Meanwhile, this same Republican Congress and the Republican president, George W. Bush, ignored their duties under our Constitution, failing to ensure border security and enforce our immigration laws. They also failed to implement an effective policy response to a rapidly emerging energy crisis; failed to take any action to fix an out-of-control health care crisis; and failed to balance budgets or ensure efficient, productive use of taxpayers' money. It is difficult to recall any examples of statesmanship or creative problem solving from this Congress. Overall, I saw a complete betrayal of the conservative Founding Fathers' values by my own Republican Party.

It was due to this rapidly deteriorating political crisis and my great concern for the welfare of my two young children and their generation that, in 2005, I began hosting a conservative call-in radio show in Orlando, Florida, *A Different Direction*. The show challenged listeners to consider the nation's pressing problems in relation to our Founding Fathers' values and principles and to propose solutions, rather than just another "curse the politicians" in Washington show.

I quickly learned how many others shared my concerns and values, desperately looking for statesmen to replace career politicians. Spurred on by this and seeing the absence of any statesmanlike leadership in my own congressional district, I decided to challenge the Republican incumbent Ric Keller in the August 2008 Republican primary as a candidate for the congressional seat in the Eighth District of Florida. (See Appendix for my congressional candidate experience.)

Despite losing the race, I emerged with an even stronger conviction that the values and principles of government set forth by our Founders were correct and that the solutions to America's challenges based on these values, as well as the lessons I learned during the campaign, could be usefully shared through the vehicle of a short book.

As President Reagan reminded us, "All great change in America takes place at the dinner table."[5] I know that we ordinary citizens can solve the tremendous challenges our nation is now facing, just as the Founding Fathers and President Reagan overcame the challenges of their day. The way forward is to employ their same values, fighting spirit, and perseverance. At the moment, however, America is sliding down the path toward socialism. The good news is that more and more Americans are beginning to wake up to this impending disaster and are demanding new leadership that will adhere to our nation's original principles of government. This fact is evidenced by the outbreak of Tea Party demonstrations (Taxed Enough Already) throughout the nation.

I firmly believe that now is the time for conservatives to reform the Republican Party, and revive our Constitution and the values of our Founders. We can and must win the battle for the soul of America. We have history and truth on our side. No other system of values and government principles has ever come close to working as well as the ones established by our Founders.

With these objectives as my goal, I will examine our Founders' values and how they have been abandoned. I will analyze how President Barack Obama and our institutions—including a career-politician Congress, the U.S. Supreme Court, misleading liberal media, a failing public school system, an apathetic Christian Church, and an irresponsible, uninformed citizenry—have been destroying this nation's foundation. Most importantly, I will provide specific solutions to our nation's most pressing domestic challenges based on the Founders' principles and lay out a plan for the one hope we have of preserving our great nation—a "Conservative Comeback."

★ *Part I* ★

AMERICA'S CHANGING VALUES

1

The Wisdom of Our Founding Fathers

*I have always believed that America is
strongest and freest and happiest when it is
truest to the wisdom of its founders.*

—President Ronald Reagan[1]

LIKE PRESIDENT REAGAN more than thirty years ago, I strongly believe America must return to our Founding Fathers' values and principles of government to solve successfully our great national challenges, so let's first look back at the values for which the early patriots fought and died; values which enabled America to become the world's freest, wealthiest, and greatest nation for more than two hundred years.

Throughout our history, and especially during times of crisis and conflict, these values and principles so beloved by our forefathers have served us well, both as inspiration and as guidance. In 1825, reflecting on what the fathers of our country had bequeathed to the new generation of national leaders then coming of age, Daniel Webster observed that, "We can win no laurels in a war for independence. Earlier and worthier hands have gathered them all. Nor are there places for us as founders of the states. Our fathers have filled them. But there remains to us a great duty of defense and preservation."[2]

The phrase *Founding Fathers* has been attributed to then-Senator Warren G. Harding, who used it in his address to the 1916 Republican National Committee. The term has come to include the signers of the Declaration of Independence, the Constitution, and other founding documents, and other persons who participated in the American Revolution as leaders of the

9

patriots. Notable among them were George Washington, Thomas Jefferson, John Adams, James Madison, John Hancock, Benjamin Franklin, and Alexander Hamilton.

The Founding Fathers collectively represented a broad spectrum of ages and Christian denominations. They were God-fearing men of various educational backgrounds, professions, and experiences. They were not infallible; many were slaveholders. What united them, however, transcended their differences and frailties. First and foremost was their love of freedom and a shared commitment to protect the hard-won liberties Americans had sought ever since the first refugees from political and economic oppression landed on this country's shores. They were determined to enshrine and protect for perpetuity the freedoms that had been won with so much blood and sacrifice: freedoms of religion, speech, assemblage, the press, to bear arms, and to pursue one's happiness without excessive taxation or government interference.

From the outset, the Founding Fathers struggled to construct the type of government that would provide greatest assurance that the freedoms and values they cherished would be protected and maintained. Their challenge was to create "one nation under God," without sacrificing to a central authority the individual rights and obligations that from the time of the Pilgrim fathers had been vested in the people and their individual states.

In 1786, the Continental Congress met in Philadelphia to revise the original Articles of Confederation to grant Congress the power to collect taxes and regulate foreign commerce. The allocation of power that emerged, after days of contentious debate between federalists and those who feared a centralized government, created a new form of government, which was enshrined in our Constitution. It was unprecedented in the history of mankind. On that occasion, indicative of the fragile accord that had been struck, Benjamin Franklin responded to a question from a lady as to what type of government the nation had, stating famously, "A Republic, if you can keep it."[3]

Over the next 225 years, more than a million Americans have

heroically fought and died to preserve the values, principles, and institutions established by the Founding Fathers against both external and domestic threats. The core values and principles became, in particular, the foundation for "conservatism" as a political philosophy in America. Over the years, conservatism came to be associated with the Republican Party. It represented a distinct philosophy of limited government, capitalism, and an emphasis on freedom and personal responsibility that contrasts it with the collectivist's urge toward big government and centralized power that advocates wealth redistribution and government control.

Thomas Paine exemplified the spirit of the great men and women who formed our country. On one critical occasion in our nation's history, General George Washington ordered that his soldiers at Valley Forge be read a portion of Paine's essay, *The Crisis*, for inspiration when he feared that many of them were beginning to think their cause hopeless. It included the following call to action, which should be indelibly etched in the hearts and minds of American leaders today and in the future: "If there must be trouble, let it be in my day, that my child may have peace, and this single reflection, well applied, is sufficient to awaken every man to duty."[4]

As illustrated by both the words and deeds of Paine and Washington, the Founders focused on their responsibilities to the nation and their children, not just on their rights. Early Americans revered God, the Bible (which was taught in many of our public schools), the traditional family, hard work, and personal responsibility. Our Founders also realized that this unique republic could only succeed if its laws and values were based on the values of the Bible, while at the same time affording everyone the right to practice his own religion or no religion at all.

Here is a little known fact: almost one-half of the fifty-six signers of the Declaration were seminary graduates.[5] God and the Bible were central to their belief system and lay at the heart of the laws that were enacted in those early days. One has only to consider the words of our earliest presidents to gain appreciation of the importance they attached to these values:

> Religion and morality [based on the teachings of the Bible] are indispensable supports of this self-government.
> —GEORGE WASHINGTON, FAREWELL ADDRESS, 1796 (AUTHOR'S PARAPHRASE)[6]

> Our Constitution was made only for a moral and religious people. It is wholly inadequate to the government of any other.
> —JOHN ADAMS, SECOND PRESIDENT[7]

> We have staked the whole future of American civilization not upon the power of government, far from it. We have staked the future of our political institutions upon the capacity of mankind for self-government; upon the capacity of each and all of us to govern ourselves, to control ourselves, to sustain ourselves according to the Ten Commandments of God.
> —JAMES MADISON, FOURTH PRESIDENT, PRINCIPAL AUTHOR OF THE U.S. CONSTITUTION[8]

Do politicians talk like this anymore? Certainly, no one in the Democratic Party, and far too few in its Republican counterpart, do. In fact, when President Barack Obama stopped in Turkey during his first European tour as President, he felt compelled to opine that the U.S. "is no longer a Christian nation,"[9] despite the fact that many of the Founders stated just the opposite and the fact that the U.S. Supreme Court for the first 150 years of America's existence stated in its opinions that we are a Christian nation!

In the Founders' days, the only constraint on religion and Christianity (the dominant religion of the people) was found in the First Amendment: "Congress shall make no law respecting an establishment of religion, or prohibiting the free exercise thereof." Because of the Founders' tremendous respect for states' rights, the states were permitted to deal with religious issues as they saw fit.

Bible teaching was common in the public schools. Over the last fifty years, however, the teaching of the Bible in our schools, along with school prayer and especially any expression of Christian faith, has been taken from Americans not because of any amendments to the Constitution or because of the will of the people, but solely as a symptom of rampant political correctness and its outright disrespect for the Constitution, states' rights, and citizen rights by the modern U.S. Supreme Court.

Along with remembering our Constitution, we must also reacquaint ourselves with the spirit and content of the Declaration of Independence, which set forth the Founders' values. The Declaration is for our nation what an Article of Incorporation is for a business. Both establish who is forming the group, and the name, purpose, and function of the body being formed and the activities in which it may engage. In the Declaration, the Founders described the rights they believed God had given to all men. At its core are the following assertions and commitments:

> We hold these truths to be self-evident, that all men are created equal, that they are endowed by their Creator with certain unalienable Rights, that among these are Life, Liberty and the pursuit of Happiness. [Author's note: a "Right to Health Care" does not appear.] That to secure these rights, Governments are instituted among Men, deriving their just powers from the consent of the governed. That whenever any Form of Government becomes destructive of these ends, it is the Right of the People to alter or to abolish it and to institute new Government...And for the support of this Declaration, with a firm reliance on the protection of Divine Providence, we mutually pledge to each other our Lives, our Fortunes, and our sacred Honor.
> —THOMAS JEFFERSON, 1776

It is extremely important to note that the Founders specifically stated in our Declaration of Independence that the only purpose of government was to secure God-given rights of "Life, Liberty and the pursuit of Happiness"—not to redistribute wealth or determine what it believes is fair. They set up the federal government to protect them from foreign threats, to guard the nation's sovereignty, and to make certain that no one, including the states, violated their God-given rights. Another reason the Founders established a limited federal government was that citizens did not expect the federal government to do much for them. The Founders envisioned a nation of self-reliant individuals who are enriched, educated, and inspired by their own efforts and achievements alongside their fellow citizens.

In drafting our Constitution and Bill of Rights, the Founders were determined to protect the states from unwanted interference or control by the federal government. With firsthand knowledge of how power corrupts both people and governments, they took numerous steps through the brilliance of checks and balances in our Constitution and Bill of Rights to make sure power would be disbursed primarily to the governed, the individual citizens and their states. The Founders were determined to safeguard the new nation and its citizens from power-hungry kings, central governing authorities, and politicians who might decide at some point to try to limit or subvert individual freedom and liberty.

In short, the Founders of our nation were statesmen first. They were driven by freedom and the protection of God-given individual rights. They worked hard and with tremendous courage to build a strong, free, and lasting country. These men and women risked their lives for their beliefs and for the betterment of their children and future generations. We are the fortunate beneficiaries of their wisdom and selflessness. Our children deserve the same from us.

2

Abandoning Our Heritage

*The first principle of totalitarianism is that the State is competent to
do all things and is limited in what it actually does only by the will
of those who control the State. It is clear that this view is in direct
conflict with the Constitution, which is an instrument above all
for limiting the functions of government....The Founding Fathers
had a reason for endorsing this principle of limited government.*

*Throughout history, government has proved to be the chief
instrument for thwarting man's liberty. Government represents
power in the hands of some men to control and regulate the
lives of other men. And power, as Lord Acton said, corrupts
men. "Absolute power," he added, "corrupts absolutely."*

—Former United States Senator Barry Goldwater[1]

Secularists, liberals, many career politicians, judges, academics, and the media now disdain the wisdom expressed by our Founders and Senator Goldwater. I think we would be forgiven for occasionally wondering whether some secretly despise our Founders' values; but at minimum, much of the political Left clearly ignores our Constitution until it supports their agenda. During the health care reform and global warming debates, one prominent liberal commentator went so far as to openly admire the supposed ease with which the ruling communist party of China inflicts its policies on the Chinese people, apparently due to the absence of a pesky democratic system that allows the governed population to actually vote and choose. Of all the things the collectivists and liberals are, shameless certainly is not one of them.

In his 2006 book, *The Audacity of Hope*, then-Senator Barack Obama wrote, "I have to side with Justice (Andrew) Breyer's view of the Constitution, that it is not a static but, rather, a living document and must be read in the context of an ever-changing world."[2] Translation: "We will do with this document as we please, including ignoring it or re-interpreting it to meet our agenda." How comforting that philosophy would be to our Founders.

Today's Congress does not acknowledge the constitutional restraints upon its power to tax and spend. It also shows no foresight or shame in taking actions that will bankrupt future generations. At the same time, year after year we witness self-serving, power-hungry career politicians voting themselves large salaries with ever-larger annual raises to go along with comfortable lifetime pensions, while taking perks and privileges from lobbyists at the same time. Too many use their elected positions not to uphold our Constitution and promote individual freedom, but to increase their own wealth, importance, and fame.

Likewise, the modern Supreme Court has completely disregarded the Constitution in numerous ways, including its *Roe v. Wade* decision, disregarding states' rights, removing prayer and Bible studies from our public schools, and granting Congress unlimited power to tax and spend for any purpose. The Court has turned the Constitution of our country, which limits the federal government's power and protects individual freedom, into an almost meaningless document while giving itself, Congress, and the federal government vast, unlimited powers. Meanwhile, our educational system fails to effectively teach our children the principles set forth in the Declaration of Independence and the Constitution. The values expressed by our Founders are no longer studied or taught in our public schools to the degree necessary so that each generation may understand our Founders' principles and values.

The nation's media are also a big part of the problem. Other than a few radio talk show hosts like Glenn Beck, they rarely, if ever, discuss how our Constitution is a document intended to greatly limit the federal government's power. Meanwhile, they continue to mislead the public into believing that principles like "separation of church and state" are found in the Constitution, and that increasing tax rates is necessary to increase tax revenues. They rarely search for truth and then objectively report facts. Instead, they spread and re-spread their opinions with nothing of substance to support them, as they advocate for big government and the abandonment of our Founders' values.

Contrast our Founders' values with the modern liberal media's vision of an America full of "subjects" dependent on the government for handouts. Liberal policies dictate that the state confiscates and redistributes wealth and limits liberty for society's own good. Some liberals appear to see and to treat their fellow citizens as cash cows to be milked. Some are motivated by wealth envy, seeing other individuals' wealth as the cause of their own poverty. As a result, they disdain the very people who work hard and create the wealth that establishes a great economy, lifts people out of poverty, and pays for the bottomless pit of new government programs to which they have been addicted since Roosevelt's New Deal.

Consider our friend Boris in the following story:

> There were two Russian peasants, Ivan and Boris, who were alike in all ways except one. Ivan had a pet goat that gave him companionship and milk. Boris always resented this. One day, Boris' luck changed. While he was walking along the road, he found a bottle. When he uncorked it, a genie appeared, thanking Boris for releasing him after three thousand years, and telling him that as a reward Boris could have any wish he wanted. After thinking about this for several minutes, Boris said, "I wish that Ivan's goat would die!" (Author's paraphrase)[3]

This idea of thinking only about punishing others, like Boris did, rather than trying to improve your own lot in life is too often

17

found in the liberalism on display today; it is exemplified by those excited at the prospect of seeing the wealthy forced to pay higher taxes under the Obama administration.

> You cannot strengthen the weak by weakening the strong.
>
> —RONALD REAGAN
> 1992 REPUBLICAN NATIONAL CONVENTION
> (ORIGINALLY BY REV. WILLIAM BOETCKER, 1916)[4]

As a result of all of these forces over the last sixty years, our children have grown up ignorant of their responsibilities as Americans to be self-reliant and of the limitations the Founders placed on our federal government. In the more than two hundred years since our nation settled on the principles that unite us, we have forgotten our roots and abandoned the values on which the United States was built. We now have a society afflicted with an entitlement mentality, and with little sense of what freedom is really all about.

> Liberty not only means that the individual has both the opportunity and burden of choice; it also means that he must bear the consequences of his actions. Liberty and responsibility are inseparable.
>
> —F.A. HAYEK[5]

The effects of the abandonment of our Founders' values are obvious. Look at California's liberal culture and what a disaster the state has become today, despite its spectacular natural beauty and beaches, abundant natural resources, and favorable climate. Currently, California has accumulated more than $500 billion in debt[6] and its businesses and achievers are leaving the state in droves. Formerly, it had a strong industrial base, exemplified by Silicon Valley. Now, it has one of the nation's highest unemployment rates.

For years, California encouraged millions of illegal immigrants to settle there by giving them jobs and billions in benefits. It has encouraged a welfare society and many of its citizens reject all of the Founders' principles, including the traditional Judeo-Christian values. California has continually raised taxes on its citizens. It has the nation's fourth-highest state income tax rate and incurred steadily more debt to pay for a massive welfare system.

As a result, California is looking to other states' taxpayers to bail it out. Fortunately for its residents, the Democratic Congress bailed them out through President Obama's $787 billion "stimulus" program. Despite billions of dollars in federal taxpayer relief, it may take decades for California to recover, if it ever does, because it has so badly violated most of our Founders' values. In the meantime, its failures will drag down other innocent taxpayers as our federal government ignores the Constitution and forces the rest of us to clean up California's mess! Congressmen Barney Frank proposed a bill whereby California bonds would be secured by the federal government (i.e. the American taxpayer). This way, if California defaults again, we taxpayers pick up the tab for the benefits California's own residents are unwilling to pay for.

On the national level, look at what former President Jimmy Carter and a Democrat Congress did to this country in the late 1970s and early 1980s. His presidency featured high taxes and an emphasis on wealth redistribution, and it helped cause double-digit inflation and 20 percent interest rates, high unemployment, and a crippling recession. I know liberals and the media want to pretend this Carter recession never occurred and, therefore, represent today's recession as the worst since the Great Depression. The truth is, however, the Carter recession was far worse in many of the ways I just mentioned. The result of that infamous liberal president's attempt to redistribute wealth was that the poor got poorer and everyone else just got poor!

In 2006, the American public once again forgot about liberalism's repeated failures and voted for a democratic, liberal Congress, with Nancy Pelosi and Harry Reid to run their economy. The results— once again—have been spectacular, wouldn't you say? There is a worldwide economic recession, an unemployment rate of 10-plus percent, and deficits for 2009, 2010, and 2011 beetween $1 and $2 trillion. We have massive corporate and union bailouts, with President Obama and our Congress doing away with free-market capitalism in favor of artificially picking winners and losers. The big banks, United Auto Workers, General Electric (which owns the Obama praise networks NBC and MSNBC), ACORN, and other friends and allies of the Democratic Party receive billions from the government, some for doing nothing except failing.

Government benefits such as Social Security, food stamps, unemployment insurance, and health care in the first quarter of 2009 accounted for 16.2 percent of Americans' personal income,[7] the highest percentage ever in American history. All of this is done at the expense of other taxpayers and future generations, who, in one form or another, will all have to pay for this "free money," not to mention the damage done to freedom, national security, and the rule of law.

Conservatism vs. Dependency

I N THE 1960s, Senator Barry Goldwater from Arizona spearheaded a resurgence of the conservative political movement in America and, in so doing, became known as "Mr. Conservative." In his widely read book, *The Conscience of a Conservative*, Goldwater observed that:[1]

> The root difference between the Conservatives and the Liberals of today is that Conservatives take account of the whole man, while the Liberals tend to look only at the material side of man's nature. The Conservative believes that man is, in part, an economic, an animal creature; but that he is also a spiritual creature with spiritual needs and desires...
>
> Surely the first obligation of a political thinker is to understand the nature of man...The first thing he has learned about man is that each member of the species is a unique creature. Man's most sacred possession is his individual soul—which has an immortal side, but also a mortal one...Secondly, the Conservative has learned that the spiritual aspects of man's nature are inextricably intertwined. He cannot be economically free, or even economically efficient, if he is enslaved politically; conversely, man's political freedom is illusory if he is dependent for his economic needs on the State.
>
> The Conservative realizes, thirdly, that man's development, in both its spiritual and material aspects, is not something that can be directed by outside forces. Every

man, for his own individual good and the good of his society, is responsible for his own development.

Four decades later, Senator John McCain (from Arizona as Goldwater was, but hardly a conservative in the same mold) astutely described conservative values and beliefs as follows:

> They (Americans) want their government to operate as their families operate, on a realistic budget, with an eye on the future that spurns self-indulgence in the short term for the sake of lasting prosperity, that respects hard work and individual initiative, and that shows no favoritism to one group of Americans over another....
>
> We believe in work, faith, service, a culture of life, personal responsibility. We believe in the integrity and values of families, neighborhoods and communities. We believe in limited government in a federal system, individual and property rights and finding solutions to public problems closest to the people....
>
> Common-sense conservatives believe that the government that governs least governs best, that the government should do only those things individuals cannot do for themselves and do them efficiently.[2]

It is difficult to imagine our Founding Fathers disagreeing with any of these beliefs and values; nor, I venture to say, would most clear-thinking Americans today. Yet these uniquely American, time-tested values are presently under assault by liberal elements in our society who condemn capitalism for its faults, question the capacity of individual citizens to make the right choices, and believe that the heavy hand of a large, omnipotent federal government is required to set things right.

We have seen the bankruptcy of the liberal approach in the past and we are seeing it today with the Obama administration acting in lockstep with a Democratic-controlled Congress. One terrible consequence of unlimited federal government power is corresponding unlimited dependency that springs from it. Just as with drug addiction, more and more of our citizens are becoming "hooked" on public handouts. As they demand more and more from government, they demand less and less of themselves. This hurts everyone in our society. One thing is for sure—never in American history have the people demanded so much from their government and so little from themselves.

At a town hall meeting, one attendee asked President Obama for help:

> I was making $3,000 a month and now have been laid off and am only getting $1,100 a month from unemployment. Why can't you just bump it up to $3,000 until I get a job?[3]

President Obama's reply—an echo of what he consistently replies to requests for government assistance—was, basically, "We are going to help you and everyone else in your condition through extended unemployment coverage, increased benefits, and an assortment of other government programs" (author's paraphrase, not directly quoted).

The media always responds to these "excellent questions" about an individual's difficult circumstances with nodding approval and then presses our politicians even harder to state what exactly the federal government is going to do to respond. I bet that if this question had been posed to George Washington, Ben Franklin, John Adams, or Thomas Jefferson, their reply to this man would have gone along these lines:

> You're getting $1,100 from whom? Why is the federal government taking money from one citizen who is working and giving it to you, who is not? That is not freedom. We never gave the federal government that power. Did the American people amend the Constitution and agree that

the federal government may redistribute wealth if and when it wants to?

Won't such a transfer lead to many people working less if they can do nothing, yet still get the government to take income from someone else? How does society create wealth and a good standard of living for its people when people do not have to work to survive? Will hard workers or achievers still want to live in this country and take risks to create wealth and jobs when a powerful few can just confiscate their hard-earned wealth for any reason?

With respect to welfarism, Goldwater suggested that we all:

Consider the consequences to the recipient of welfarism. For one thing, he mortgages himself to the federal government. In return for benefits—which, in the majority of cases, he pays for—he concedes to the government the ultimate in political power—the power to grant or withhold from him the necessities of life as the government sees fit. Even more important, however, is the effect on him—the elimination of any feeling of responsibility for his own welfare and that of his family and neighbors. A man may not immediately, or ever, comprehend the harm thus done to his character. Indeed, this is one of the great evils of Welfarism—that it transforms the individual from a dignified, industrious, self-reliant spiritual being into a dependent animal creature without his knowing it. There is no avoiding this damage to character under the Welfare State. Welfare programs cannot help but promote the idea that the government owes the benefits it confers on the individual, and that the individual is entitled, by right, to receive them.[4]

Many people would immediately say Goldwater and folks like me who agree with his reasoning are cold and unsympathetic to the plight of the poor. They might agree with the general theory that capitalism and less government is good, but feel that in real life there are so many people with difficulties that we must use the federal government to provide for everyone. Many of my fellow Christians naively believe that because the Bible repeatedly emphasizes our duty to minister to the poor, the federal government through its taxing power is the right instrument to carry this out. For some reason, it has to be the federal government taking care of the poor rather than states, communities, churches, charities, or other individuals.

Who do you think can most effectively, efficiently, and lovingly attend to the needs of the poor and disabled and better enable the poor to fulfill their responsibility to work hard and utilize all of their skills to become prosperous? Who can best do this job without stealing from our children? The answer is painfully obvious, but we now have a federal government attempting to fulfill this role and, as a result, our nation risks being crushed by a culture of laziness, inefficiency, corruption, fraud, and debt!

To the extent that government has a role to play in the realm of social welfare, it exists at the state and local levels, much closer to the citizens who are at risk. Ministering from Washington, D.C., is the worst of all approaches. Hard-earned taxpayer dollars are wasted and society is victimized by corruption, overhead, and inefficiency. There is little accountability, and our children wind up with an unimaginable debt—heading as high as *$14 trillion!*—supposedly in the name of compassion. Bad government is bad government is bad government!

Moreover, real compassion is giving one's own time and money to someone else. It is not having the government confiscate someone else's money to transfer it to other individuals it judges to be worthy. There is nothing compassionate about politicians engaged in wealth redistribution to gain power and wealth.

If the big-government welfare enthusiasts in the Democratic Party want people like me to take them seriously when they proclaim their compassion for the poor and needy, they need to start "walking the walk."

President Obama, for example, gave between $1,000 and $3,400 a year to charity according to his tax returns from 2000 through 2004.[5] During this period, he was making about $240,000 a year, which meant he was so concerned about the poor, needy, and underprivileged that he saw fit to give between .4 and 1.4 percent of his income to charitable causes, including his church.

Below are his reported tax returns:[6]

Year	*AGI	Charitable Gifts	Gifts/AGI
2006	$983,826	$60,307	6.1 percent
2005	$1,655,106	$77,315	4.7 percent
2004	$207,647	$2,500	1.2 percent
2003	$238,327	$3,400	1.4 percent
2002	$259,394	$1,050	0.4 percent
2001	$272,759	$1,470	0.5 percent
2000	$240,505	$2,350	1 percent

* adjusted gross income

Our number two in command, Vice President Joe Biden, gave $3,690 to charitable causes in ten years (an average of $369 a year) from 1998 thru 2007, or .2 percent of his income according to his tax returns![7] During this same period, he was chastising Republicans, big business, and others making the same income for being so uncaring and selfish.

Here are Biden's charitable contributions for the years covered by the tax returns:[8]

Year	AGI	Charitable Gifts	Gifts/AGI
2007	$319,853	$995	.31 percent
2006	$248,459	$380	.15 percent
2005	$321,379	$380	.11 percent
2004	$234,271	$380	.16 percent
2003	$231,375	$260	.11 percent
2002	$227,811	$260	.11 percent
2001	$220,712	$360	.16 percent
2000	$219,953	$360	.16 percent
1999	$210,797	$120	.06 percent
1998	$215,432	$195	.09 percent

Meanwhile, a 2005 study by the Center on Philanthropy at Indiana University revealed that people making $200,000 to $500,000 a year (like Obama and Biden) contributed an average of $40,000 a year to charitable causes.[9] Let's see: $40,000 contributed by the average person versus $2,000 for Obama and $369 for Biden. Obama contributes 5 percent and Biden less than 1 percent of the average charitable contribution for their income bracket. Tell me again, President Obama, about collectivism and how "we all" need to take better care of one another—or does "spreading the wealth around" only apply to other people's money?

When President Obama first took office, he proposed taking away tax breaks for individuals' charitable contributions for people making more than $250,000 a year. Can someone explain to me why he wants to take away people's incentive to give money to charitable causes, particularly when our recession is already causing so much hardship for these institutions already? One can only surmise President Obama does not want anyone helping the poor except the government so he can further control them and their votes.

It is fair to ask whether the Democratic Party really is the champion of the poor, or if it caters to the poor as the means to collect ever greater wealth and power? I know this much: these so-called champions of the poor are getting rich and powerful while receiving votes, money, and praise from the poor. The truth is that the liberal high tax and big-government-spending philosophy causes the poor to stay poor and government-dependent, with little or no self-worth or sense of personal achievement, generation after generation after generation, as Democrats continually tell them they cannot make it in this world without the government's help.

One reason President Obama repeatedly emphasizes the importance of words is that he needs people to focus on his words, and not his deeds, which rarely match. He should be judged on his actions and policies, not his words. Words are often used to manipulate and deceive, and often are hollow and self-serving, particularly from politicians.

The primary reason I am a conservative is that conservatism, based on free-market capitalism and personal responsibility, provides the best mechanism for moving the poor out of poverty and helping them to achieve their potential. How do you believe that America became the wealthiest nation in the world, creating in the process the highest standard of living experienced by the largest number of people anywhere else on the planet? How did we manage to lift so many people out of poverty to the point where even the poorest American lives a better life than 90 percent of the world's population? And why, even at a time when we are in a recession and America's way of life is treated with scorn by leaders, politicians, and media in other nations, do we still see so many poor people throughout the world fleeing to the U.S.? We owe it all to people who embraced freedom, hard work, and capitalism.

The reason so many people desire a heavy involvement by Washington is obvious. While they may not be able to articulate how a big central government with high taxation helps the nation's economy—because it doesn't—they do believe the government "freebies" will help their personal economy. Too many (nearly 40 percent of Americans) do not have to pay for these programs since they do not pay federal income taxes.[10] Does it bother them that somebody else had to drag themselves out of bed, perhaps even working two jobs, to pay for their benefits? No, their thinking seems to be that if the government prints money or takes it from kids they have never met or are not born yet, well, who cares? That's their problem! I got mine! This is the entitlement mentality in a nutshell, created and fertilized for more than four decades by the welfare state.

Unfortunately, our Congress, and too many of our citizens, are embracing a "me first" mentality, with a tremendous appetite for entitlement, rights, and privileges hand-in-hand with a corresponding diminished feeling of personal responsibility. We apparently now have a right to free health care and other massive government benefits with no responsibility to feed or take care of ourselves and our children. Most depressingly, this message is repeatedly ingrained into the minds of our children through our failing education system.

You may think this book is tough on people. It is meant to be tough, to encourage the very best in all of us. America was intended to be a free nation of self-reliant achievers, not a nation in which our government drags us down to the lowest common denominator. Freedom is about governing ourselves, not receiving handouts. Tough love is what this nation needs. We all need to take a second look at what we ask of our federal government and what we ask and expect of ourselves. Do we really want the responsibility that goes with freedom? The Founders answered, "Yes!" I hope that will be our answer. To paraphrase one of President Reagan's keenest observations, "We don't celebrate 'Dependence on the Government Day' on July 4th, we celebrate Independence Day!" (author's paraphrase).[11]

4

RE-ESTABLISHING THE FOUNDERS' VALUES

I'll lay me down and bleed awhile. Though I am
wounded, I am not slain. I shall rise and fight again.
—RONALD REAGAN, AFTER LOSING THE 1976
REPUBLICAN PRESIDENTIAL NOMINATION[1]

THE PRESIDENTIAL ELECTION of 2008 and the opinion polls taken during and after provide stark evidence of how far conservatism and the Republican Party have fallen in the eyes of the American public. It has reached the point where political pundits and authors are now addressing the question, "Is conservatism dead in America?"

We conservatives cannot turn away from the considerable challenge this presents. The stakes for our nation are too high. Instead, we must pick ourselves up, as Ronald Reagan did three decades ago, and reclaim the high ground in American politics. And, in keeping with the thesis of this book, we can look to the past to find our way through the present and onward into the future. President Abraham Lincoln gave us the basic guideposts we need:

> Intelligence, patriotism, Christianity and a firm reliance
> on Him, who has never yet forsaken this favored land, are
> still competent to adjust in the best way all our present
> difficulty.[2]

How conservatism had reached this present-day low ebb is not difficult to understand. There is blame enough to go around. First, "conservatism" is equated in the public's eye with the Republican Party. As Republican lawmakers and administrations in recent years have abdicated the conservative principles of small government, balanced budgets, individual freedom, individual responsibility, and respect for the rule of law, true conservatives have been dragged down with it.

We even had the Bush administration professing to wear the mantle of the "compassionate conservative" and, in so doing, conveyed to the American public that earlier conservatives lacked compassion. The Founding Fathers, Ronald Reagan, and thousands of conservative leaders who came earlier must still be spinning in their graves.

We conservatives also have ourselves to blame. Why were we asleep while the Republican establishment was sidelining our values for the party? Why were we not recruiting and actively supporting primary challengers in the Republican primaries to take on big government and ineffective leaders? Why did we turn our children over to the liberal public school system and universities, to be misled and lied to about so many critical economic issues and truths about our Founders' values without recognizing the long-term consequences for our nation?

Accordingly, we cannot succeed and pass on a great nation to our children without all of us doing our part to ensure that the public understands our Founders' principles of government. At the local level, the Declaration of Independence and Constitution must be read and studied by our students in both our middle and high schools.

Equally important to our nation's prosperity is that every child must be taught basic economic principles. First and foremost is the fact that government cannot create wealth and therefore cannot lift people out of poverty. Only individuals, operating in freedom and working hard, being innovative, and taking risks can provide a high standard of living for the nation's citizens and lift people out of poverty. This simple fact is not being taught and few of our citizens reflect on this timeless and all-important principle.

President Obama loves to state that we need to, "rebuild this economy from the bottom up."[3] The comment always draws cheers and is a classic example of him misleading his approving audience. Governments cannot build an economy; individuals build economies. Governments can only destroy economies and destroy wealth-creation. Many socialist governments do just that. If someone would like to explain to me how a government is going to build an economy from the bottom up or when this has ever been done successfully in the history of mankind, I'm all ears! The more amazing fact is that when President Obama utters this nonsense, no one in the media or the Republican Party ever challenges him on it.

Conservatives must also change their rhetoric from the outdated and ineffective "less taxes and less government" argument. We must become problem solvers, which means advocating for wealth-creation and job-creation policies combined with specific budget cuts. This, of course, means we must first stop supporting our current tax code which taxes wealth-creating activities and production and instead support taxing consumption to once again make America the most business-friendly nation in the world. (See Chapter 7, "Our Dysfunctional Tax Code and the Fair Tax Solution" for details about the Fair Tax.)

We must also fight relentlessly to ensure that all Americans continuously receive a historical perspective on the past success of America's capitalism. As we know, there are too many politicians, educators, media members, and liberal elements encouraging America to become a socialist nation. They must be countered by pounding home the point, among other arguments, that their remedies have been tried before, to the sorrow of all affected, by Marx, Engels, and other socialists who followed. While I realize liberals and many media members like to bypass the facts and go straight to their opinions, *facts matter!* It is the lack of knowledge that largely explains why people vote as they do, and why our country's prosperity and freedom are so threatened.

The April 15, 2009, tax-day Tea Party protests held in more than

170 cities and which drew hundreds of thousands of protesters were very encouraging. Clearly, many Americans want us to return to our Founders' principles and are ready to fight in a much more passionate and aggressive manner. The Tea Party protesters recognized how both parties have failed America and how far astray from America's Constitution and founding principles the Congress and President Obama are now taking this country. The Tea Party movement is calling attention to the inevitable, disastrous results that will surely follow from continuing on this path.

Having participated with my family in several Orlando Tea Party rallies, it was heartwarming to see the great concern average Americans had for their nation and future generations. I am very proud to be a part of such a noble cause. Translating this passion into fighting successfully for new conservative leaders in Congress will be a defining moment for this grassroots movement.

There are other very promising signs that conservatives are responding to the federal government's abandonment of our Constitution and founding principles. Glenn Beck's "9/12 Project," which promotes our Founders' values and asks his listeners to support them, has galvanized hundreds of thousands more to the cause, while his book, *Common Sense*, is a number-one best seller.

Further, conservatives are now beginning to challenge entrenched career-politician incumbents in Republican primary U.S. Senate races. Faced with such a challenge from conservative Pat Toomey, liberal-leaning Arlen Spector (Pennsylvania) left the Republican Party to keep his seat. In Florida, former State Speaker of the House Marco Rubio, a strong supporter of the Founders' values, is taking on the epitome of the liberal Republican, Governor and career politician Charlie Crist, for the U.S. Senate seat vacated by Senator Mel Martinez.

Let me digress and discuss the importance of the Florida race because I believe it will be a defining moment for the "conservative comeback" in our nation. I strongly encourage everyone to support Marco Rubio if you believe in our Founders' principles, or if you are tired of career politicians who have no constructive solutions to problems, but enjoy the perks and privileges of power, such as current Governor Crist who was supported of President Obama's $787 billion stimulus program and advocated very publicly for its passage. He recently appointed a liberal Democrat to the Florida Supreme Court because he wanted diversity. He is in favor of Obama's "cap and trade" bill, opposes increased drilling for oil and natural gas off Florida's coast because of global warming concerns, and has consistently raided Florida's trust funds meant for future generations to solve his short-term budget problems. While Florida was sinking into recession in 2008, he took a lavish taxpayer-funded trip to Europe[4] and followed John McCain around hoping to become Vice President instead of solving any of the state's numerous challenges.

Meanwhile, former State Representative Marco Rubio is a young, articulate, passionate advocate for social and economic conservative values, capitalism, tax reform, and balanced budgets, and will be a national star once he gets elected. The Crist–Rubio primary will be the first great battle for the soul of the Republican Party.

Here's the truth: our nation can survive a liberal Democratic Party, as it has for many decades now. America will always be filled with people who demand handouts from government; that is, they want the government to take other people's hard-earned income and give it to them. Meanwhile, liberals seeking power, at the expense of the poor they purportedly care so much about, will always be here with clever rationalizations and word games to justify their flawed philosophies. The good news is that whenever liberals have come to power in the past, the great majority of people quickly realize that their principles and policies do not work.

What this country cannot survive, however, is a corrupt, value-less Republican Party run by career politicians and self-serving special-interest groups. That is the situation we currently face and it presents our nation with an extreme crisis. Very few are even aware that this will be the defining challenge of our time. The elected establishment of the current Republican Party must be broken up and replaced by statesmen who revere God, limited government, freedom, and wealth-creating capitalism, who will be vigilant stewards of future generations' money.

Our party needs to be led by citizen legislators dedicated to protecting the Constitution and a decentralized government. As Ronald Reagan said, "Concentrated power is always the enemy of liberty."[5]

The current Republican congressional leaders, many of whom have been in Congress far too long, have no credibility with the American people. They squandered their opportunity from 2001 to 2006 when they had complete control of the federal government. Now, most deserve to be voted out of office.

P.J. O'Rourke was proven right when he famously stated:[6]

> The Democrats are the party of government activism, the party that says government can make you richer, smarter, taller and get the chickweed out of your lawn. Republicans are the party that says government doesn't work and then get elected and prove it.

This is why, my Republican and conservative friends, you should not be worried about Pelosi, Reid, and Obama, but much more concerned about your party being run by big business, lobbyists, the illegal-immigration-supporting U.S. Chamber of Commerce, and career politicians whose incompetence and abandonment of our Founders' values gave our country over to the Democrats in the first place. Misguided Republican leadership and an apathetic citizenry will destroy this nation, not Democrats being Democrats.

I suggest that going forward we let the Democrats explain why they are willing to bankrupt the nation's children to pay off special-interest groups that fund their campaigns, while Republicans truly fight for less spending and balanced budgets. Leave the Democrats to explain why they are the party of career politicians, while

Republicans—offering specific solutions to problems—go to serve without privilege for a few years and return home. When the youth see this selfless commitment to their future, they will start voting Republican, as they did when Ronald Reagan was president and Republicans were winning younger voters by twenty-point margins. People will always respond to the truth coming from people who truly care about them.

To accomplish our goals, we must continually make it clear to the public that the 2001–2006 Republican Congress had nothing to do with conservatism. We must also be able to articulate to everyone that conservative values are the values of the Founders, which Reagan again proved to be successful.

Richard Viguerie, the president and author of *Conservatives Betrayed* (a conservative Web portal and book of the same title), provided us with words of wisdom regarding conservatives mounting a comeback to regain control of their government. Viguerie believes that conservatives should reform the Republican Party rather than form a third party. Viguerie further suggests that we no longer think of ourselves as Republicans, but as Reagan conservatives.

Viguerie believes, and I agree, that we withhold support from the Republican National Committee because it routinely spends money in primaries to defeat conservative candidates. There is nothing more important we can do for our country than to begin challenging these incumbent, big-government Republicans in every race, and support underdog, solution-oriented conservatives with all our resources.

Primary challengers do not receive the special interest Republican support, no matter how abysmal the incumbent opponent. As a result, they need our money and all of us to volunteer to get their message out to the public. I promise you that without a concerted effort to defeat these entrenched incumbent Republicans in the primaries, this nation cannot turn around and we will have failed our country.

Finally, we Reagan conservatives must nominate a candidate for president in 2012 who is passionate about the Founders' values, is a man of great character, and has specific solutions to our nation's challenges. I believe that man may very well be former Arkansas Governor Mike Huckabee, who did an outstanding job for his state with a Democratic legislature. He understands wealth creation (thus supports the Fair Tax), has a deep concern for all people, and a great reverence for our heroic military and our Constitution. We all have our favorites, but I only ask that you consider his accomplishments as governor; look into why he was named Governor of the Year; and examine his values and solutions to problems if he runs again. I also like someone who can accomplish a lot with very little money, such as Huckabee's campaign did, a trait we desperately will need in the White House in 2012.

Regardless of your own preference, however, the time has come for all of us to be far better stewards of our country. Now is not the time to despair or to sit back and complain about liberals who seek to further advance their agenda. Rather, it is time to rediscover our fighting spirit, the same spirit that allowed the Founders to overcome tremendous odds and build this great country.

Having revisited our values and principles, let's now look at the critical issues currently facing our nation and consider how specific conservative solutions can and must be the basis on which our challenges can be dealt with successfully.

★ *Part II* ★

PUTTING AMERICA'S FINANCIAL HOUSE IN ORDER

5

The Road to a $12 Trillion National Debt

*A democracy cannot exist as a permanent form of government.
It can only exist until the voters discover that they can vote themselves largesse from the public treasury. From that moment on,
the majority always votes for the candidates promising the most
benefits from the public treasury with the result that a democracy always collapses over loose fiscal policy, always followed by a
dictatorship. The average age of the world's greatest civilizations
has been 200 years... Great nations rise and fall. The people go
from bondage to spiritual truth, to great courage, from courage to
liberty, from liberty to abundance, from abundance to selfishness,
from selfishness to complacency, from complacency to apathy, from
apathy to dependence, from dependence back again to bondage.*
—Alexis de Tocqueville, 19th century
French philosopher[1]

C AN ANY AMERICAN today read de Tocqueville's analysis
of the fate of democracies without a feeling that he was
completely on the mark—and we must change course
immediately? Thanks to loose fiscal policy in combination with
growing dependency on government spending and moral decline,
our national indebtedness has now reached $11.5 trillion,[2] growing
by $3.8 billion each day![3] The government's outstanding obliga-
tions, including promises to retirees, has risen to a beginning figure
or at least $65 trillion.[4] Read that again—sixty-five *trillion* dollars!

What is a trillion dollars? Chris Martenson's online "Crash
Course" in economics explains a trillion this way: first, picture
a million dollars as a four-inch stack of thousand-dollar bills. A
comparable billion-dollar stack is 358 feet tall. A trillion-dollar

41

stack of thousand-dollar bills stands 67.9 miles high. One would need a stack of thousand-dollar bills 740 miles high to reach 11 trillion![5]

Our annual interest payment on the national debt is now $202 billion, and that is with interest rates extremely low.[6] Can you imagine what these payments will cost when interest rates start rising? The Concord Coalition estimates that in ten years we may be making interest payments of $750 billion or more each year.[7] Fortunately for many Americans, this is a case of out of sight, out of mind—just make sure to fund my program!

Our slide down the path toward government dependency, socialism and, ultimately, to bondage has been swift. How did this happen? What can we do to prove de Tocqueville wrong? Let's examine the facts, recognizing that our national debt depends, one, on our economic growth, and two, on government expenditures.

For the nation's first two hundred years, the U.S. Congress did a very good job of balancing budgets. For most of this period, we had very limited federal government spending because no one expected anything from the federal government except protection of certain God-given rights, but certainly not benefits and handouts. This began to change with the emergence of President Franklin D. Roosevelt's "Great Society" in the 1930s.

In 1977, when President Jimmy Carter took office, actions taken by Carter and a Democratic Congress started to dramatically increase the deficit. The national debt quickly rose from more than $600 billion to almost $1 trillion in four years, an increase that equaled that of the prior 27 years,[8] and we were off to a new era in American government. By 1989, our debt had grown to nearly $2.9 trillion after two terms of President Reagan and the then-constant Democratic Congress.[9] Some of the indebtedness was due to laudable expenditures, consistent with our Constitution's mandate to promote the general welfare and provide for our common defense.

In the 1980s, President Reagan greatly increased defense spending, which helped win the Cold War without having to fire a shot. The

Soviet Union's centralized economy collapsed as a result of loose fiscal policy, trying to keep up with capitalism and Reagan's large military budget, growing nuclear arsenal, and the Strategic Defense Initiative missile defense program. Meanwhile, Reagan was unable to reduce other domestic spending as the Democratic Congress, led by House Speaker Tip O'Neill, agreed to Reagan's large tax cuts and massive defense spending only in return for the increased domestic spending that the Democrats wanted.

In the 1980s, President Reagan's conservative leadership and tax cuts also led the way to a booming economy, which greatly lowered double-digit inflation rates, interest rates, and unemployment; conditions that had dominated President Jimmy Carter's four years from 1977 to 1981. Interestingly, America's revived economy also increased government's tax revenues, despite Reagan's significantly lower tax rates. This does occur quite frequently, contrary to media and liberal repeated assertions that increasing tax rates is the only way to increase tax revenues.

After President Reagan's leadership produced victory over the Soviets in the Cold War, America received a "peace dividend" as we were able to reduce defense spending during President Bill Clinton's two terms from 1993 to 2001. No rational person would argue that defeating the Soviet Empire, with its nuclear capability, liberating Eastern Europe, and providing our nation with a tremendously sophisticated and strong military was not money well spent.

Beginning in 1989, with the national debt at less than $3 trillion, a Democratic Congress, President George H. Bush, and then-President Bill Clinton dramatically increased domestic spending and ran large deficits of hundreds of billions annually for far different reasons, including expanded individual benefits, subsidies, earmarks, and new government programs.

Respect for fiscal responsibility eroded rapidly. Only a few seemed to notice or care. One who did was Texas billionaire Ross Perot. In 1992, Perot emerged on the national political scene as an Independent candidate for president. He perceptively warned us of the consequences of Congress's loose fiscal policy and our tremendous national debt. Due in part to Perot's efforts, important legislation to address these challenges was almost passed during President Bill Clinton's two terms in office, including a Balanced Budget Amendment to the Constitution (which, unfortunately, failed by one vote in the U.S. Senate). During this period, a presidential line item veto was passed, but then ruled unconstitutional by the U.S. Supreme Court, which held that it gave too much legislative power to the president.

With the deficits continuing to rise dramatically in Clinton's first term, Perot ran for President again in 1996 and his voice continued to put pressure on the Congress to balance budgets. By the end of Clinton's second term, he and a Republican Congress, led by the Speaker of the House Newt Gingrich, had balanced the budget (by the U.S. Government's measure). Their calculations did not, however, include Congress' raid on our Social Security funds and government pension funds.

Contrary to the views of revisionists and those with bad memories, President Clinton and the Congress dramatically increased the national debt during his eight years, from $4.1 trillion to $5.7 trillion, despite the strong U.S. economy and large tax revenues.[10] The economic growth was fueled in large part by the stock market's "dot.com" bubble before it collapsed at the end of Clinton's second term.

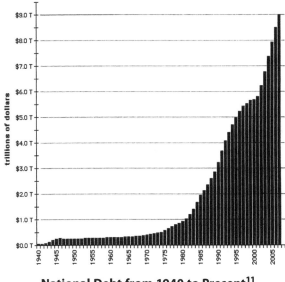

National Debt from 1940 to Present[11]

It is important to note that the Clinton and Reagan presidencies each increased the national debt by about the same amount, $1.7 trillion,[12] but Reagan built a great military, helped bring freedom to millions of Eastern Europeans, and made the world much safer with the collapse of the Soviet Empire.

In 2000, conservatives helped elect a Republican-controlled Congress and President George W. Bush based in part on their promises of fiscal responsibility and restrained government spending. This supposedly conservative Republican Congress and President instead proved to be among the most fiscally irresponsible leaders in our nation's history. The national debt ballooned from $5.7 trillion to $8.5 trillion[13] before the Republicans lost power to the Democrats in both houses of Congress in 2006.

Why did the debt go out of control? It certainly was not a lack of taxes being collected or poor revenues. During the six years from 2001 to 2006, tax revenues actually reached an all-time high, increasing from $2.1 trillion to $2.56 trillion, despite President George W. Bush instituting a series of significant across-the-board tax-rate decreases following the 9/11 terrorist attacks.[14] Facts matter—or they should, if you want your country to be successful. How many people in this country do you think know that tax revenues went up, not down, after Bush's tax-rate cuts?

From 2001 to 2006, the nation enjoyed low unemployment, low interest rates, and a housing boom. Just as in the Clinton years, this was an easy period to balance budgets, with large tax revenues and baby boomers in their peak earning years. Bush and the Congress, however, greatly increased spending on virtually all government programs at a pace not seen since the Great Depression and FDR. This included adding a new, massive program for prescription drug benefits for seniors, tens of billions in annual farm subsidies, and tens of billions in earmarks, while our nation tried to fund wars in Iraq and Afghanistan.

In the 2006 elections, Democratic congressional leaders Harry Reid and Nancy Pelosi decried the budget deficits, promising a new era of fiscal responsibility if only the people would give Democrats control of Congress. Instead, after becoming the majority party in 2007, the Democratic Congress ran even higher budget deficits and, in fiscal 2008, passed a budget with the highest one-year deficit, $454 billion, of the entire Bush presidency.

An important point to consider is that government-reported budget deficits are often not close to the real deficit total. In their accounting, they never include the hundreds of billions that our government borrows each year from Social Security taxes, federal-employee pension funds, and the interest it pays on all our debt (with IOUs, not cash). For example, *USA Today* reported that the 2008 deficit was actually $1 trillion, as opposed to the government-reported $454 billion.[15] By late 2008, the Democratic Congress continued to hyper-spend with a $700 billion Troubled Assets Recovery Program (otherwise known as the TARP Program), a $787 billion "stimulus" bill, and a $410 billion Omnibus spending bill, which, according to the Congressional Budget Office (CBO), will lead to a nearly $1.8 trillion deficit in 2009 alone![16] The national debt is now more than $12 trillion.[17] This means in effect that each citizen now owes nearly $40,000, and a family of four owes almost $160,000 for all the government debt and unfunded promises already made.[18] What is more shocking and irresponsible is that the Democrats believe that is not nearly enough debt. In February 2010 the Democrat Congress voted to raise the national debt limit ceiling to more than $14 trillion causing more deficits well in excess of $1 trillion. They fight to explode our debt with more programs and bailouts every day, including their program to socialize our health care industry that likely will cost trillions more over the next ten years. Further, the CBO predicts that President Obama's latest budget proposals for the next ten years would add another $9.3 trillion to our national debt,[19] in addition to the existing debt.

Deficit (in billions)[20]

Deficit	Year
-$459	2008
-$1,845	2009
-$1,379	2010
-$970	2011
-$658	2012
-$672	2013
-$749	2014
-$785	2015
-$895	2016
-$949	2017
-$1,023	2018
-$1,189	2019

Deeper in debt
President Obama's preliminary budget plan would add $9.3 trillion in debt from 2010 to 2019, according to a Congressional Budget Office estimate.

Now the states are following suit and no longer paying their bills. In the first three months of 2009, states and local governments borrowed $53.5 billion.[21]

The national debt mounts at a dizzying pace each day just as 78 million baby boomers start retiring, which will cause our debt to skyrocket that much faster. This is happening in a country already losing its manufacturing base while much of its prized real estate and many of its banks and corporations are now owned by foreigners. Instead, America mostly just borrows and consumes. I wonder how all this printing of money will turn out. How can one even comment on something so clearly suicidal?

At some point, with the printing of hundreds and hundreds of billions that our Treasury is engaged in and the unlimited borrowing, the value of our dollar will sink enough that hyperinflation and shockingly high interest rates will become a strong possibility causing unthinkable suffering for all Americans. Our dollar has already lost value dramatically since 2001 when this extreme borrowing first began. Have you noticed how your dollars now buy far less health care and education for your kids, and gas for your car? And this is mainly since 2001 when the national debt has expanded from 6 to $10 trillion. Remember this every time the government prints money and hands out "federal dollars" to some interest group or creates another program.

China and Japan each hold close to $1 trillion in American government debt[22] and are now looking with skepticism at President Obama's plan to print and borrow trillions more and ramp up more debt to unheard-of levels. China's Prime Minister Wen Jiabao has stated on more than one occasion that he is very worried about the ability of the U.S. to repay its debt. As a result, China is now starting to only make short-term loans (buy short-term bonds) to the U.S. as they see the very real possibility of a collapse of the U.S. dollar. One thing seems clear: unless we dramatically change course, no matter what careers our children choose, they are going to be working for the government to repay the Chinese and other lenders!

Here are a few other key facts regarding government spending and our national and personal debt:

- Government spending on benefit payments will exceed $2 trillion in 2009.[23]
- If all outstanding $65 trillion-plus[24] of total federal obligations were met, Americans would have to pay a minimum of nearly $217,000 each.
- In 1956, 60 percent of spending was for national defense and 22 percent on individual payments. By 2006, it had reversed, with 20 percent of spending on defense and 60 percent on individuals.[25]
- Approximately 50 percent of our debt is now owed to foreign interests, compared to 1970 when foreigners owned only 5 percent of the U.S. debt.[26]
- In 2007, household debt (including mortgages) totaled $13.8 trillion, while in 2000 that figure was $6.9 trillion.[27]

6

A 12-Point Plan to Reduce Government Spending and Balance the Budget

The principle of spending money to be paid by posterity under the name of funding is but swindling futurity on a large scale. It is incumbent on every generation to pay its own debts as it goes, a principle which, if acted on, would save one-half the wars of the world.

—Thomas Jefferson[1]

THE FOLLOWING IS a summary of my twelve-point plan for dramatically reducing government spending and ensuring balanced budgets:

1. Pass a Constitutional Balanced-Budget Amendment that would require Congress to balance budgets.
2. End illegal immigration.
3. Eliminate the Department of Education and other federal departments unnecessary to fulfill the federal government's limited role as authorized by our Constitution.
4. For younger workers (age fifty-five and under), gradually raise the eligibility age for Social Security and Medicare to seventy since life expectancy has increased fourteen years since Social Security was established. The goal should be to ensure the permanent solvency of the two programs, while protecting the benefits of those currently enrolled and those nearing retirement age. Alternatively, privatize Social Security for younger

workers, as set forth in Chapter 16 "Entitlement Reform."

5. End bailouts.

6. Cut health care costs through mandatory physical fitness and nutrition programs in schools, which Congress would require of any state asking for Medicaid money.

7. Pass a revised Presidential Line-Item Veto bill that satisfies the Supreme Court.

8. End earmark spending.

9. Eliminate mismanagement, waste, and fraud in our federal government through continuing review by independent oversight agencies, with increased funding and other incentives for cost management, particularly for the Defense Department, Medicare, and Medicaid.

10. Legislate and assess severe criminal penalties for anyone who defrauds taxpayers, including public officials.

11. Cut congressional salaries by 5 percent after each year they do not balance the budget until a constitutional amendment to balance budgets becomes law.

12. Amend the Constitution to provide for term limits for Congress and ban former Congressmen from lobbying the federal government after leaving office to eliminate much of the incentive to overspend.

The Citizens Against Government Waste (www.cagw.org) has put out a complete list of specific cuts that would save the U.S. $2 trillion over five years. I encourage everyone to view this list, if for no other reason than to remind us of the large number of poorly conceived, wasteful, and ineffective taxpayer-funded programs mandated by our Congress.

7

Our Dysfunctional Tax Code
and the Fair Tax Solution

*I predict future happiness for Americans if they can
prevent the government from wasting the labors of the
people under the pretense of taking care of them.*

—Thomas Jefferson[1]

I T IS CERTAIN that to begin solving our national debt problem
and ensure we have a healthy economy that produces good-
paying jobs for Americans, we need a tax system that works.
An essential fact that every adult should recognize, and every child
should be taught, is the following: to create wealth and provide
its citizens with a good standard of living through good-paying
jobs, a nation *must* have economic and tax systems that encourage
individual investment, hard work, and productivity. It must also
incentivize business owners to take risks, rather than deterring this
activity. If you tax productivity, you are going to get less of it. That
is common sense.

Let's consider our current tax system and my hero, Ed Barnett
of Wichita Falls. He wrote a letter to radio show host Glenn Beck
as follows:

Dear IRS,

I'm sorry to inform you that I'm not going to be able to pay
the taxes owed on April 15th, but all is not lost. I paid these
taxes: accounts receivable tax, building permit tax, CDL
tax, corporate income tax, dog license tax, federal income
tax, unemployment tax, gas tax, hunting license tax, fishing

license tax, waterfowl stamp tax, inheritance tax, inventory tax, liquor tax, luxury tax, Medicare tax, city tax, school and county property tax (up to 33 percent the last four years), real estate tax, Social Security tax, road-use tax, toll-road tax, state and city sales tax, recreational vehicle tax, sales franchise tax, state unemployment tax, federal excise tax, telephone tax, telephone (federal, state and local) surcharge tax, telephone minimum-usage surcharge tax, utility tax, vehicle tax, registration tax, capital-gains tax, lease-severance tax, oil-and-gas assessment tax, Colorado property tax, Texas, Colorado, Wyoming, Oklahoma, Mexico sales tax, and many more I can't recall and I've run out of space and money. When you do not receive my check April 15th, just know that it was an honest mistake. Please treat me the same as the way you've treated Congressman Charlie Rangel, Chris Dodd, Barney Frank, ex-Congressman Tom Daschle and, of course, your boss, Timothy Geithner. No penalties, no interest.

P.S.: I'll make at least a partial payment as soon as I get my stimulus check.

Ed Barnett

Wichita Falls[2]

Ed, I'm with you, buddy. You did not even mention the embedded taxes, which dramatically raise the cost of all the goods we buy, since corporations pass on these taxes to the consumer. Nevertheless, Ed, according to President Obama and the Democrats, you are still holding on to too much of the "government's money."

Good-bye Founding Fathers' freedoms and our prosperous America—hello, socialism!

Who pays the federal income taxes under our current system?[3]

WHO PAYS INCOME TAXES? SEE WHO
PAYS WHAT FOR TAX YEAR 2006

Percentiles Ranked by *AGI	AGI Threshold on Percentiles	Percentage of Federal Personal Income Tax Paid
Top 1 percent	$388,806	39.89
Top 5 percent	$153,542	60.14
Top 10 percent	$108,904	70.79
Top 25 percent	$64,702	86.27
Top 50 percent	$31,987	97.01
Bottom 50 percent	<$31,987	2.99

* adjusted gross income

The U.S. Tax Code is sixty thousand pages of Internal Revenue Service rules and regulations. Most of it seems designed by Congressmen for Congressmen who use the code to secure and acquire power and to reward industries and businesses that fund their campaigns.

Even special-interest groups not given special favors cater to the incumbents for fear that their industries and businesses will be harmed by the ability of the Congress to pick winners and losers through the tax code. There are thousands of tax breaks, favors, and loopholes the public has no idea even exist. These favors result in a very powerful Congress, with very little turnover, tens of thousands of wealthy lobbyists, and special-interest groups and certain businesses given special treatment over ordinary Americans. With each new funding bill or stimulus package, the code expands.

Our tax code is so complicated that it costs taxpayers billions of dollars annually to comply with the regulations. According to the

National Taxpayers Union, in 2002, individuals, businesses, and non-profits spent 3.5 billion hours trying to understand, comply with, and, too often, to manipulate the tax code.[4] Compliance costs are estimated at $28 billion annually.[5] Why should American taxpayers be punished in this manner so that Congress can hand out favors in return for campaign contributions? The absurdity of this complexity is highlighted by the fact that our U.S. Treasury Secretary, Timothy Geithner, did not pay some of his taxes back in 2001 through 2004 because, according to him, he did not understand the rules.[6]

In 2001, more than $290 billion in taxes was not collected, due to fraud and the complexities of the ridiculous system.[7] If President Obama's Treasury Secretary cannot comprehend the code, no one else should be expected to be able to comply, either. Just as we saw in the financial crisis of 2008, the more complicated the mortgage-backed securities became, the more complicated Congress made the tax codes. The result was hardly a surprise—more fraud and abuse, and less chance for the public to have any idea of what was actually happening.

One undeniable fact regarding our republic is that our federal government should not be favoring certain groups over others. Therefore, taxpayers deserve a system that is fair, transparent, and simple; with the present, outrageous tax code, we have strayed very far from this principle. For example, many corporations in the U.S. are paying the second-highest corporate rate in the world (35 percent), while others pay zero or very little because of tax breaks and loopholes created by their political influence. Congress has created breaks for favored industries that could total more than a trillion dollars over the next decade. The top twenty hedge fund managers in 2007 earned an average of $657 million each, but paid only a 15 percent capital gains rate on their income because of tax loopholes.[8] Other job-creating citizens who do not even make $1 million are paying 35 percent. Worse yet, millions of illegal immigrants in the underground economy, criminals who deal in cash and many others who enjoy government benefits provided by the hard-working taxpayers, do not pay any income taxes under our current system.

We have a system that is not only unfair, but also discourages investment and savings by taxing capital gains and interest income. Everyone agrees that it is important for our citizens to save money; yet, wide areas of the country borrowed money from their home equity lines and credit cards and accumulated no savings for several years until that trend began to turn around early in 2009. It is, therefore, insane to tax interest on savings and checking accounts or on investments in stocks and mutual funds, as responsible, hard-working people try to accumulate savings for their retirement, particularly when Social Security is going broke!

When most of the country has their 401(k) retirement funds in mutual funds, why should we tax capital gains and at the same time make it so much harder for American businessmen to invest in their companies and succeed? I thought we wanted the stock market to go up, businesses to be successful, and employ millions of Americans—not punish people who try to start and grow businesses, and those trying to responsibly save for retirement so they do not have to be dependent on government.

Our tax code also discourages productivity and entrepreneurship through progressive tax rates on income, as well as through the corporate and payroll taxes. This nation is losing millions of jobs overseas each year to countries with lower taxes, cheap labor, and fewer regulations. Why in the world would we want to chase corporations and businesses away through such heavy taxes?

The progressive tax rates on individuals penalize individuals who want to work hard while discouraging people from working two jobs. People who are willing to take risks and start their own businesses, which help create so many of our jobs, are disincentivized and discouraged when 50 percent of their income is going to the government through various taxes to redistribute their wealth.

Does anyone really believe our nation's citizens are going to benefit and be able to compete in this global economy if we have high corporate tax rates, capital gains taxes, payroll taxes, income taxes, property taxes, sales taxes, and a myriad other taxes? Why would successful businesses set up shop here? All of these taxes presently make the U.S. a terrible country in which to locate your business or keep your money. Businessmen are not dumb. They will always head to favorable business climates in tax-friendly states and countries.

Just look at what happened to states like Michigan, and specifically a city like Detroit that has been run exclusively by Democrats. Detroit taxes its population heavily, caters to unions, and in general, creates an unfavorable business climate. Since 1950, Detroit has lost half of its population (from 1.8 million to 900,000)[9] and now features a 14.9 percent unemployment rate.[10] From 2000 to 2005, when times were good, Michigan still suffered six straight years of job losses.[11] Michigan is now a mess—it has the nation's highest unemployment rate at 14.7 percent as of late 2009, a dubious distinction state has held for four consecutive years,[12] along with high taxes, destructive unions, and little to no economic growth. And the rest of our country is headed in much the same direction.

Consider what happened in Maryland. In 2007, the Democratic legislature passed a bill, effective 2008, to create a higher tax bracket for millionaires to generate more tax revenues. Proponents said the change would bring in more than $100 million in additional revenue. They made their tax code more progressive, the age-old liberal approach. The result one year later was that the number of Marylanders who filed and paid those extra taxes dropped by one-third and tax revenues collected fell more than $100 million from this group.[13] Clearly, some people left the state and others took steps to avoid the tax. You will not hear those facts on the nightly news or discussed on America's college campuses.

Rather than continuing this wealth strangulation policy of high taxes to support massive government programs and spending, President Obama and Democrats around the nation would be much better off if they would heed the wisdom of their hero, former President John F. Kennedy, when he said this about capitalism and big-government tax-and-spend policies in his 1963 State of the Union address:

> It is increasingly clear—to those in government, business and labor who are responsible for our economy's success— that our obsolete tax system exerts too heavy a drag on private purchasing power, profits and employment...It discourages extra effort and risk. It distorts the use of resources. It invites recurrent recessions, depresses our federal revenues and causes chronic budget deficits.[14]

Why is it so difficult for our politicians and media to recognize that the last four times the marginal tax rates have been reduced, the amount of revenue taken in by our Treasury has actually increased? Coolidge cut marginal tax rates in the 1920s; Kennedy cut them in the 1960s; Reagan cut them in the 1980s; and Bush cut them in 2001–2005. In each case the economy expanded, bringing with it a larger base for taxation and, hence, larger tax revenues.

Facts do matter.

It is pitiful that so many in this country continue to believe that raising tax rates will automatically increase tax revenues despite consistent evidence to the contrary. This notion is one of the great liberal lies. However, if the truth ever got to the masses of this historical fact, the class warfare arguments liberals rely on would no longer serve their purpose.

This is some of what we have to show for our current tax code, with its massive taxes and other government policy:

- Unemployment has reached 10-plus percent[15] with more than 15.3 million out of work,[16] the highest in nearly thirty years.
- Foreclosures could reach between 6.5 million and 8 million by 2012.[17]

Given the massive problems with our tax code, I have become an ardent supporter of the Fair Tax. This reform of our tax system has been made popular by conservative radio show host Neil Boortz, who, together with Congressman John Linder, wrote two books on the subject. In the 2008 presidential campaign, Governor Mike Huckabee of Arkansas was a strong advocate for this approach and it already had a large national network of passionate supporters. A bill to implement the Fair Tax has been introduced in both houses of Congress (H.R. 25 on January 6, 2009, and S. 296 on January 22, 2009) and has more than sixty-three co-sponsors.

The Fair Tax was created by a group of leading economic experts who tried to figure out the most practical tax system for our country, one that would not hurt the poor, and would be fair and simple, while helping create wealth and raise the standard of living for all Americans. In a nutshell, the Fair Tax proposes the elimination of all federal taxes, including income taxes, taxes for Medicare and Social Security, capital-gains taxes, corporate taxes, self-employment taxes, gift taxes, and estate taxes. They would be replaced by a twenty-three-cent sales tax on new goods and services at the retail level. This change would require a constitutional amendment to repeal the Sixteenth Amendment, which allows the federal government to tax our income. Please note that when the Founders formed this nation, they did not tax income. The federal income tax became a permanent feature of our tax code only in the 1900s.

In fact, imagine for a moment everyone being able to keep his/her entire paycheck with no tax deductions and retaining 100 percent of all profits on investments in American businesses. How much do you think Americans' productivity would increase? How much more motivated would people be to work hard or start a new business and employ people if they could keep the fruit of their labor instead of giving 50 percent to the government in taxes? How much more would we invest and save if none of our investment, capital, or savings gains were taxed? Nearly one in three Americans have investment accounts with brokers, so I think it is safe to say that Americans need the stock market to do well and that removing capital gains taxes would be a great short-term *and* long-term stimulus that would not cost our children a penny.

Right now, there are trillions of Americans' dollars sitting in offshore accounts specifically to avoid paying these brutal U.S. taxes. Imagine if we moved to the Fair Tax tomorrow and witnessed that money begin to flow back into our economy. *That would be real stimulus—with no downside!*

In a recent survey, six hundred overseas business leaders were asked what they would do if our country eliminated all these taxes and switched to the Fair Tax. Forty percent said that the next plant or office they opened would be located in the U.S. The other 60 percent said they would shut down their existing operations a.s.a.p. and move to the most tax-friendly country in the world—the U.S.! (author's parahrase)[18]

I will not attempt to write a "Fair Tax Book" or answer every question regarding this proposal. But I am convinced that this plan will work and will be a win/win for everyone.

First, let's consider how we will pay our bills if we cut all the current taxes mentioned earlier. The Fair Tax plan is designed to generate the same level of tax revenues by broadening the tax base. Illegal immigrants, the underground economy, and others who currently escape paying taxes would all contribute under the Fair Tax. Research on this concept showed that a twenty-three-cent sales tax on new goods and services would generate the same revenue as under our current tax code. Moreover, the obvious growth in our economy would eventually spur added revenues through increased productivity and a much more prosperous nation for all.

One very important benefit from the Fair Tax would be the elimination of the massive embedded taxes we pay, the "silent killers." We Americans rarely, if ever, think about the hidden taxes built into the prices of the goods we buy. Businesses, obviously, have to pass all of these taxes (e.g., corporate and payroll taxes for Social Security and Medicare) on to the consumer in the form of higher prices. With the Fair Tax, these embedded taxes disappear and the prices of goods and services naturally come down. As a result, even with a twenty-three-cent sales tax under the Fair Tax, the prices of the goods and services will rise very little, if at all, and all of that would be offset by the reduction in price from the elimination of the "silent killer" taxes.

Consider the effect of these embedded taxes on U.S. manufacturers trying to compete in today's global economy. They cannot compete having to pay all these taxes, particularly when other countries like India, China, or Japan have cheaper labor rates and less regulation. If we are serious about competing successfully globally and having a strong manufacturing base, we must rid our businesses of these embedded taxes.

Republican Congressman Steve King of Iowa addressed the tremendous job-creation benefits of the Fair Tax when he appeared on my radio show *The Conservative Comeback*. Referring to the current plight of the U.S. automakers, he observed how much lower their costs would be and how much more cheaply they could sell a car and still make a profit if the embedded taxes the industry now faces under our current system could be eliminated.

Since foreign automakers do not pay any such embedded taxes, they have a substantial advantage over U.S. automakers, which not only face a punishing tax code but also the weight of higher wages, health care costs, and retirement benefits. With the Fair Tax, both foreign automakers and U.S. automakers would be competing on a much more level playing field. American consumers would experience higher costs for foreign cars with the twenty-three-cent sales tax, but much lower costs on American cars. Further, the U.S. taxpayers would not be paying the more than $50 billion to bail out the domestic auto industry.

I share Representative King's mystification as to why the American autoworkers do not push hard for the Fair Tax to save their jobs and industry. What is clear is that their Democratic leadership hates the idea of losing power and not being able to force all of these taxes on people to pay for their government programs.

With respect to the poor, the Fair Tax plan features a *prebate* mechanism, providing a check each month from the government to every single adult or family in the amount of the additional sales taxes on necessities up to the poverty level. Under the Fair Tax prebate, a single person would receive $188 per month and a married couple with no children would receive $376 per month. In addition to the prebate, the poor and everyone else will no longer have Social Security or Medicare taxes withheld from their paychecks. This would result in an immediate 25- to 30-percent increase in everyone's take home pay.[19]

There are two big losers under the fair tax—politicians and lobbyists! They will no longer be able to use our tax code to maintain and enhance their power and wealth. Imagine a Congress actually forced to do its job of governing!

> Our federal tax system is, in short, utterly impossible, utterly unjust and completely counterproductive, [it] reeks with injustice and is fundamentally un-American…it has earned a rebellion and it's time we rebelled.
> —PRESIDENT RONALD REAGAN[20]

In summary, the Fair Tax would provide a large and immediate stimulus to our economy, while raising Americans' standard of living over the long term. Secondly, thousands of lobbyists would return home from Washington and power would be transferred back to the people and away from career politicians and special-interest groups. Thirdly, there is little risk associated with this proposal because we do not raise nearly enough revenues to pay our bills under the current system. Finally, there would be the elimination of the IRS as we have known it, making April 15th just another day. It sure sounds good to me. Let's help Americans create true wealth, lure business back to the U.S., and unleash and reward productivity and risk-taking like never before.

The political establishment, for the most part, hates the idea because it will render useless their power source: lobbyists and special-interest groups. I believe, before the 2012 presidential election, our Republican Party should be forced to decide whether it is going to be a defender of the current tax code or switch to the Fair Tax. For a party with no solutions for a middle class that cannot pay rising health care and/or tuition costs, or for the disappearance of American jobs, the choice is obvious to me, as I believe it would be to the Founding Fathers.

I encourage all of you to become active in promoting the cause. If you have not already, read Neil Boortz' Fair Tax books, which answer a lot of valid questions and natural concerns regarding the proposal. Look for information on his Web site: www.thefairtax. org. I also encourage you to join a local Fair Tax group through their Web site and become active. Fair Tax rallies are held everywhere in major cities throughout the nation.

Make sure your congressmen and senators are co-sponsors of the Fair Tax Act (H.R. 25 or S.296) and are passionately promoting its passage. If not, let's find new conservatives who are not looking for lifetime careers in Congress, who will support the Fair Tax, balanced budgets, and good economic policy that keeps the money and the power with the people. I believe one of the greatest gifts we can give our children and ourselves would be to pass the Fair Tax.

President Obama's Big-Government Agenda and Response to the Recession

The inherent vice of capitalism is the unequal sharing of blessings; the inherent virtue of socialism is the equal sharing of miseries.

—Winston Churchill[1]

P RESIDENT OBAMA HAS chosen a response to our recession and national debt crisis that is not based on principles set forth by our Founders nor is it based on capitalism. First, let's look at how our ongoing recession began. One of the first signs of trouble occurred on September 7, 2008, when the Treasury Department stepped in and took over Fannie Mae and Freddie Mac (the Federal National Mortgage Association [FNMA, or "Fannie Mae"], and Federal Home Loan Mortgage Corporation [FHLMC, or "Freddy Mac"], respectively).[2] These two government-chartered lending institutions either insured or own more than half of the nation's $11 trillion in outstanding home mortgages.[3] With the encouragement of liberals in Congress, these two government-created entities had been purchasing or guaranteeing hundreds of billions in mortgages to people who were not in a position financially to afford a home. This occurred largely through an array of social engineering programs such as the Community Reinvestment Act (CRA). From 2004 to 2007, many people were given sub-prime loans through Fannie and Freddie, and it was during this period that home prices quickly rose to unsustainable levels. Our Congress knew this was a potentially disastrous situation. If the economy worsened and/or home prices fell, many owners would not be able to afford their homes, yet our politicians encouraged this irresponsible lending.

At the same time, large multinational Wall Street lending institutions such as Bear Stearns, Lehman Brothers, and Citigroup became involved in the mortgage purchasing market, along with Fannie and Freddie. They paid mortgage originators to give mortgages to virtually anyone willing to borrow. In turn, they then bundled complex mortgage instruments and mortgage securities to sell them around the world, making tremendous fees with every sale. The money these lending institutions made was so great and so easy that they began over-leveraging themselves, buying and selling even riskier products in the quest for ever higher profits.

This system was working great from 2004 to 2007 for all involved, as home prices continued to rise and homeowners could flip, or resell, their home (or homes) for a profit. Many other homeowners took out home-equity loans, and the borrowing cycle, and the supply of homes being built, quickly began to spin out of control. Once this cycle ended, however, many of these mortgage instruments became worthless or lost much of their value. Many lending institutions and their investors throughout the world were devastated. Lehman Brothers went bankrupt in late 2008 and Bear Stearns (which the government helped sell) became worthless. With the fall of these two lending giants, it became apparent to all that a worldwide financial crisis was upon us.

Sadly, this crisis was avoidable. From 2005 to 2007, during congressional hearings, many prominent voices warned both banking committees of Congress of the dire consequences for our financial system if these irresponsible lending practices continued. Nevertheless, U.S. Representative Barney Frank, U.S. Senator Chris Dodd, and others fought hard to ensure that these institutions remained lightly regulated and incentivized to make risky loans. The result was that the Fannie and Freddie management teams made tens of millions of dollars for themselves by passing along this "bad paper." They rewarded the politicians who allowed these corrupt practices by giving Congressmen significant campaign contributions, including President Obama, Representative Frank, and Senator Dodd.[4] Predictably, as lending requirements grew more and more lax, the prices of homes got further out of control, and soon many Americans were mortgaging their future by taking cash out via home-equity loans or flipping houses for profit.

The result of this cozy relationship and Congress's failure to act in the public's interest is that taxpayers have now spent $60 billion to save Fannie and $51 billion on Freddie, with more promised.[5]

In late 2008, the federal government also took over another major failing insurance institution: the American Insurance Group (AIG), the nation's largest insurance and reinsurance conglomerate. AIG wrote credit default swaps, or insurance contracts, worth tens of trillions (yes, *trillion*—with a *t*) so investors could hedge their bets in case any of those loans went bad. Of course, AIG did not have the trillions of dollars to secure all of these instruments if a lot of the mortgages suddenly went bad, but they took the risk anyway, all while our federal government just watched.

We know now that the mortgages did go bad and AIG ultimately imploded. In its wisdom, our government then put taxpayers on the hook for more than $100 billion to bail out AIG. Tens of billions of these dollars did not really go to AIG, but to large national and foreign banks including Bank of America ($45 billion) and Citigroup ($50 billion), and banks around the world that were owed money from AIG.

What did we get? Well, we, Mr. and Mrs. American Taxpayer, now own 80 percent of AIG, and the billions more in obligations AIG still cannot meet. We could have just loaned the money to these banks directly, at least knowing that we would get paid with interest, while holding them responsible for their bad business decisions. Instead, we just gave them the money and received, in the end, stock from a company with unimaginable losses. Our government is too good to us, don't you think?

On October 3, 2008, then-President George Bush signed

legislation, supported by then-Senator Obama and passed by the Democratic Congress, known as the Emergency Economic Stabilization Act of 2008, which created the unregulated and unsupervised $700 billion Troubled Asset Relief Program (TARP). The original purpose of TARP was to unfreeze the global credit market whereby the government would buy troubled, or "toxic," mortgages and move them off the books of banks, thereby helping to unclog and free up the credit markets. Within weeks, however, the government said it was changing course and spent $250 billion to bail out nine of the largest banks in the U.S., including Goldman Sachs, Bank of America, Citigroup, and JPMorgan Chase.

Eventually, TARP gave a few large, failing lending institutions, including AIG, Fannie, and Freddie, enormous bailouts at taxpayer expense. The Treasury Department thus far has sent hundreds of billions to certain banks supposedly to help the banks lend to consumers and businesses. Instead, the lending institutions hoarded the cash, recapitalizing themselves instead of lending, and acquiring weaker banks while spending billions on executive bonuses. Imagine that. Who possibly could have foreseen they would use these funds to get their balance sheets healthy...instead of lending it in a terrible economy? It is not exactly a mystery.

Since President Obama took office, he has continued spending this TARP money to bail out these lending institutions and AIG. He also has been spending this TARP money for many of his own interests that have nothing to do with solving a worldwide banking and credit crisis. This includes helping the autoworkers unions by bailing out GM and Chrysler to the tune of $64 billion dollars.[6] The Treasury Department is now planning on giving billions to large life insurance companies. The original purpose for TARP, as sold to the American people, has been subverted by President Obama.

Up until this time, I had always believed we lived in a free country with a capitalist economy, in which people and businesses were responsible for the consequences of their actions, good or bad.

We are all beginning to learn that our Congress and President Obama believe differently; that the government is better equipped to pick the winners and losers. Does the federal government have the authority to do this under our Constitution? Of course not. But, as we will discuss later, that is no obstacle to the current leadership.

The Treasury has also printed another $700 billion and loaned it to the Federal Reserve to buy troubled consumer loans from selected financial institutions. If these loans fail, the taxpayers will be on the hook for these losses, as well; a fact that has hardly been mentioned by the media. We now own two failing mortgage companies (Fannie and Freddie), a massive, failing insurance conglomerate (AIG), majorities in two auto companies, and have acquired significant ownership interest in some large, failing banks.

Instead of following the "rule of law" and allowing the U.S. automakers to go through Chapter 11 bankruptcy reorganization, President Obama decided to bail out the auto industry and turn ownership of GM and Chrysler over to the Democrat unions and his government. No one wants to see our autoworkers become unemployed or retirees suffer. Therefore, it is very important to our nation that we have a thriving manufacturing sector, including a healthy auto industry. However, it is unlawful and immoral to trample on the rights of secured creditors and taxpayers who are now footing the bill for the failure of the industry and the unions who helped bring down their own businesses. When speaking about his decision to close Guantanamo, President Obama attempted to defend his position, saying that the "rule of law" must be followed. Exactly right, Mr. President. I wish he would follow his own counsel!

If autoworkers or any other workers want to unionize and fight for larger salaries and retiree benefits, it is certainly within their rights. Obviously, there are significant risks for all union workers when their unions negotiate lucrative deals, like the United Auto Workers did, on wages and benefits.

As my father said to me when I was young, "Watch out what you ask for; you just might get it!" It should be no surprise now to these workers that their companies went bankrupt, as foreign competitors, unburdened by high union wages and retiree costs, entered the U.S. marketplace. The union workers largely brought this crisis on themselves. I know this much: when I have made bad business decisions, which I have, I have had to suffer the consequences and have learned from my mistakes. I suggest that is exactly the lesson the unions should now be forced to learn.

In addition to the enormous debt these bailouts are creating for taxpayers, there are other costs less tangible but equally bad. Bailouts make a mockery out of accountability and consequences for bad decisions. They reward corruption, irresponsibility, and stupidity, while discouraging good business owners, as well as taxpayers, who see what is being done with their tax dollars. This is a horrible precedent that will be hard to reverse.

Just watch how our government revenues will continue to drop. According to the American Institute for Economic Research, in April 2009, federal tax revenues plunged $138 billion, or 34 percent, from a year earlier, the biggest April drop since 1981![7] Worse yet, many Americans are going to maneuver themselves around paying federal taxes if President Obama and Nancy Pelosi are going to continue to channel this money to their friends and political allies.

Wait. There's so much more President Obama is doing to us...I mean, *for* us. He has added a $750 billion stimulus program to increase the size of government and our debt. Apparently, both were too small. Do you realize that if you spent $1 million each and every day since Jesus was born, you would have spent much less than Obama did in the stimulus program he and the Democrats have enacted? The 2009 budget deficit will be the greatest in U.S. history, by far. It is projected to be at least $1.6 trillion, according to the CBO.[8] By contrast, the entire national debt over two hundred years, from George Washington's time to 1985, was less than that! President Obama's 2010 budget calls for $3.7 trillion in spending, despite the fact that tax revenues are projected to be only one-half that amount.[9] Do you see the problem with this?

And this is just the beginning—he is just getting started with his spending programs, including universal health care. Sure, we do not have any money for it, but who cares? That seems to be the White House/Democratic Congress mentality. The President then wants to give 15 million illegal immigrants amnesty to take advantage of all of his government benefits. If passed, that would certainly be the final nail in our financial coffin, and I will be writing my next book from some country whose government is not destroying its citizens' lives!

When Treasury Secretary Timothy Geithner went to China in May 2009, he sought to convince a crowd of university students that the Chinese could continue to safely buy U.S. treasury debt. Some of the students just laughed at him. The Chinese know we are self-destructing economically.

The former Federal Reserve Chairman Alan Greenspan, and now Ben Bernanke, have been warning us for more than a decade of the disaster that will ensue if we do not start balancing our budgets. Instead of heeding these warnings, President Obama is increasing our debt to levels no one could have ever imagined and sending Geithner over to China to give speeches the Chinese find comical.

Because all of this new spending is being done by Democrats, the liberal media—big government's biggest cheerleader—is constantly telling the public, "We have to do something. We have no other choice." It is reported as if it were fact that we must spend these trillions of dollars we do not have just to get through this crisis. But how about living within our means and taking the hits for the enormous mess we created, rather than passing off massive debt to our children? How about replacing our dysfunctional tax code—which is chasing business out of the country and discouraging wealth creation—with a national sales tax to raise Americans' standard of living? How about implementing an energy policy that effectively utilizes all of our natural resources to keep the wealth we create here in the U.S. instead of spending $400 to $500 billion a year on foreign oil?

How about smart regulation of our banks and lending institutions? The federal government, under our Constitution, is given the responsibility and authority to regulate commerce, so do your job. How about a return to self-reliance and prudent spending and saving by the American people? How about more adults working harder, spending less, and conducting themselves as responsible parents and citizens in the community? How about ending illegal immigration so American taxpayer dollars stay in American taxpayer hands and those jobs our economy creates go to Americans, not illegal immigrants?

America's decline is coming to pass, as de Tocqueville predicted. It is now manifested in President Obama's promising goodies for everyone: free health care, government-created jobs, more benefits, less taxes, and even money for people who pay no income taxes and more government programs—all with no cost or effort on the part of the people. All of these promises were made despite Obama's knowing we cannot begin to pay for even our current programs.

Please tell me, after all of this President Obama fever and excitement and "Change We Can Believe In," there's more to our new president than borrow-print-spend and speeches filled with soaring rhetoric. President Bush was already doing a good job of executing that philosophy. I do not recall President Obama on the campaign trail saying that the "Change We Can Believe In" was more spending, borrowing, printing money, and accruing more debt for our children. I thought I heard something about "no more failed policies of the past," and, "I will reform earmarking," and go "line by line" through the budget to get rid of programs that do not work. Whatever happened to bringing "fiscal responsibility" back to Washington D.C.?

FIGHTING FOR CAPITALISM (WARTS AND ALL)

*Capitalism is, by far, the worst system ever
invented, except all of the others.*

—WINSTON CHURCHILL, IN AN OFT-QUOTED VERSION OF HIS MORE
FAMOUS LINE, "DEMOCRACY IS THE WORST FORM OF GOVERNMENT
EXCEPT FOR ALL THOSE OTHERS THAT HAVE BEEN TRIED."[1]

WHILE PRESIDENT OBAMA and the Congress seem intent on bankrupting the nation and giving up on capitalism, I suggest we conservatives mount a vigorous defense of capitalism. To defend its virtues, we must clearly understand what it is, why it works, and acknowledge its flaws and limitations.

There are several definitions of *capitalism*. To some, it is an economic system in which wealth, and the means for producing it, are privately owned and controlled, rather than having it in the hands of the state. Others think of it as a political system dedicated to the protection of individual rights, as the basis for human growth and national economic development; and protecting and defining these rights should be the only proper role for government.

In my view, capitalism has a critical moral dimension and should thus be vigorously defended both on moral and economic grounds. It is the only system in the world that allows and assists individuals to reach their God-endowed, full potential to reap the full benefits from their labors. Make no mistake: capitalism is not only the most compassionate economic system in the world, it is the *only* compassionate economic system in the world.

In his 1970s book *Wealth and Poverty*, George Gilder wrote:[2]

The only dependable route from poverty is always work, family, and faith.

Addressing the matter of faith, Gilder observed:

> Faith in man, faith in the future, faith in the rising returns of giving, faith in the mutual benefits of trade, faith in the providence of God are all essential to successful capitalism. All are necessary to sustain the spirit of work and enterprise against the setbacks and frustrations it inevitably meets in a fallen world.[3]

The message is simple: if you want to escape poverty, do not hate wealth and capitalism. Rather, focus on these three keys: work, family, and faith; mixed with some discipline, ambition, perseverance, and a willingness to take risks.

I sure wish we would elect a president who truly believed in these values. How about you?

Sadly, as Gilder astutely observed, it is far easier for many people to believe that wealth causes poverty. Thus, they rail against capitalism and wealth-creating achievers and producers. Liberals continually suggest that the U.S. is an economically immobile and corrupt society where the poor are only exploited. As a result, they incapacitate the poor, many of whom want to believe in this lie. On this point, Gilder observed:[4]

> Upward mobility depends, or at least is partly dependent, on upward admiration, on an accurate perception of the nature of the contest and a respect for the previous winners of it.

If you continually hear or are taught that the system is corrupt, you are not going to give it your best. In a short time, you willingly give your vote, your money, and eventually your freedoms over to liberal power seekers.

Gilder accurately pointed out the fact that the U.S. is the most mobile society in the history of the world. Families with virtually zero wealth at their outset, and very poor immigrants, built America. The Japanese living in America had their holdings confiscated and were incarcerated during World War II, and thirty years later they had higher per capita earnings than any other ethnic group in America except the Jews. Three and one-half million Jewish immigrants arrived on our shores around 1900 with an average of nine dollars in their pockets. Sixty years later, the mean income of our Jewish population was almost double the national average.[5]

On the other hand, relatively wealthy British Protestants in the U.S. were passed in per capita income after World War II not only by Jews and Orientals, but also by the Irish, Italians, Germans, Poles, and the most recent generations of black West Indians. Opportunity has always been available in our country for all ethnic groups, including African-Americans and Hispanics, to lift themselves out of poverty.

The true American story is one in which poor people from every region around the world have applied America's freedoms and free-market capitalism to rise up and create the most prosperous nation in the world, with unequaled opportunity for all. Those are the facts and they are not being taught to our children!

CAPITALISM'S WARTS

As Winston Churchill frankly acknowledged, capitalism has its faults. President Reagan concurred and remarked, "Within the covers of the Bible are all the answers for all the problems men face," not capitalism.[6] There are serious downside risks for those who, by virtue of personal disability, unfortunate family or other circumstances, ignorance, or sloth, cannot compete, or choose not to. Further, the public and private schools attended by children in wealthy families usually have better teachers and more resources. Moreover, there are more opportunities for these students to attend the best private colleges, universities, and graduate schools. Clearly, some people have more opportunities and advantages than others.

Capitalism relies on people pursuing their self-interests. It thus is open to abuses in the form of fraud, deceptive practices, and unfair dealing. It tends to lead to the rich and the privileged controlling the levers of government, creating favorable laws for themselves (see bank bailouts), and disadvantaging the poor, who often have very little political power or the resources to run for political positions. Look at our U.S. Senators and how many of them are wealthy millionaires.

Throughout the history of this nation, there have been times that unregulated capitalism has led to the emergence of destructive monopolies and cartels. While I strongly oppose a heavy-handed central government, the free-market system requires some regulation to keep the players honest and consumers safe from dangerous products and services. The Founders understood these pitfalls and in our Constitution gave the Congress the responsibility to regulate foreign and interstate commerce.

We recently saw how the system can get derailed as Wall Street executives and CEOs from Fannie Mae, Freddie Mac, AIG, and others manipulated earnings and passed around "bad paper" in the form of securitized mortgages to accumulate great individual wealth, even though their companies were actually in perilous condition. Many fraudulently took advantage of their shareholders, employees, and taxpayers as the federal government neglected to properly regulate the system.

Our Founders repeatedly stated that limited government and freedom must be protected by a moral and religious people based on biblical values, and that both components were necessary for our republic to succeed. Had either Congress or Wall Street done its job and operated in accordance with the Founders' values and principles, the financial crisis of 2008–2009 would have been prevented.

One lesson emerging from the Wall Street credit crisis is that the Securities and Exchange Commission (SEC) must be reformed. The rules must be strict, simple, and ensure that banks and other lending institutions remain fully capitalized. Many of these institutions, like Citigroup, AIG, and Fannie and Freddie should be broken into smaller units to allow for smaller companies that, if unsuccessful, can fail without wreaking havoc on the world economy.

Today, the globalization of financial markets and complex financial instruments make it too easy for con artists to operate successfully in an unregulated free-market, capitalistic system. Conservatives must be at the forefront of those who condemn such abuses. We must fight for capitalism, low taxes, and fiscal responsibility, not turn a blind eye toward corporate malfeasance, manipulation, and fraud. The public, most assuredly, will rain contempt on us, not votes, if we are seen as unwilling to take on those in the financial community whose behavior introduced us to a new vocabulary of toxic assets, credit defaults, overleveraging, and the infamous "too big to fail."

Conservatives also need to stand with those who are advocating smart regulation. At the moment, conservatives are viewed by the general public as being opposed to any and all regulation. This reputation is, sadly, correct in many cases, as some of our colleagues immediately dismiss any and all proposals for new regulation. But it is precisely in the conservative tradition to have reason-based, constructive answers such as regulation if it is smart and effective. Yes, the less regulation and bureaucratic red tape, the better. In many cases, we are certainly over-regulated, but for conservatives to oppose regulatory actions by government without offering alternatives is neither responsible nor effective.

This pet political line that "I am for less regulation" is naïve and not helpful in any respect. It is not specific. When something bad happens, like a financial crisis or environmental disaster because of a lack of oversight, our Republican leaders look out of touch and incompetent. This is politically disastrous and completely unnecessary. If we are going to argue for less regulation, let's be specific and helpful.

Having acknowledged important shortcomings of capitalism, it is worth remembering two important points: first, show me a political or economic system anywhere in the world that does not have faults and imperfections and I will champion it. I can say this with confidence, because no one has a better approach: all other systems are worse. Churchill can rest easy. Second, capitalism can be regulated effectively to make certain that it works very well for all our people. This book is dedicated to the proposition that such reform is essential and is doable.

CAPITALISM'S VIRTUES

Capitalism offers many rewards, both economic and spiritual. One of the great virtues of capitalism is it encourages everyone to study hard, work hard, and maximize his or her God-given talents. In turn, this creates increased productivity in the workplace, acceleration of technological innovation, the very best products and services for consumers, and high wages and increased employment opportunities. Through open, private markets, intense competition among businesses keeps prices down, thus greatly benefiting us consumers. Socialism and big government economic control can never provide any of these advantages.

A major, but often overlooked, benefit is the sense of self-fulfillment provided to the successful participants in the system. Families prosper as parents set good examples through their hard work and self-reliance, whether they own a business, work as a doctor or nurse, or provide computer or banking services. Government welfare programs fail miserably in producing such results. In fact, they frequently result in the opposite.

Why do we have at least 11 million illegal immigrants in our country and many more people desperately wanting to follow them here rather than heading to France, Venezuela, or China?[7] It is certainly not because they have read our wonderful Constitution or like our climate. It is due to capitalism and the many possibilities it opens up for a better life. Most people realize that America is the best place in the world for a poor person to rise up and achieve their dreams.

Why do you think all other countries are relying on the U.S. to lead the world out of this global recession? We have a 230-year history of successful capitalism, with each generation living better than the one that preceded it. That's why!

Among the rights guaranteed under capitalism is the right to fail, and individuals and businesses often do. This is not all bad. Noted economists, including Alan Greenspan, keep pointing to "creative destruction" as a major factor in the building of a strong and vibrant economy. As firms and businesses close when they find it is no longer possible to compete, newer firms emerge with better ideas, products, and services, and newer, cost-saving technologies.

The rewards for those who do compete successfully, and for society as a whole, are overwhelmingly positive and provide the basis for limitless opportunities and the high standard of living Americans of every race, creed, and color enjoy.

AMERICA'S MOVE TOWARD SOCIALISM

Despite the incredible success of capitalism, for the first time in our history, neither of our two main political parties seems to be defending capitalism. Both favored massive bailouts for Fannie, Freddie, AIG, and the large financial institutions. One party (Republican) votes for big-government spending, big borrowing, and low taxes, while the other (Democrat) prefers even bigger government spending, much larger borrowing, printing of hundreds of billions of dollars, and more and higher taxes. While they may differ on taxes, they seemed joined at the hip in their belief that it is the federal government's job to take care of us all. Moreover, one recent poll indicated that only 53 percent of Americans considered capitalism preferable to socialism.[8] I will bet that fewer than 1 percent of those people who favor socialism have ever experienced it.

Right now the economy is rapidly becoming nothing more than President Obama printing and borrowing money, while he picks the winners and losers in society. He claims to be a big fan of capitalism, but clearly has either forgotten or is ignoring the maxim that capitalism offers the freedom to fail. President Obama argues that TARP and all of the bailouts are necessary because, if we allow the failure of worldwide financial institutions and large companies with tens of thousands of employees like General Motors and Chrysler, our economy will suffer and people will get hurt.

He is partially right, because when companies fail, people do get hurt. *That is capitalism!* The bigger the company, the more people are affected. Yes, that is the way it works. Neither capitalism nor any other economic system is immune from recessions and economic downturns. Fortunately, in a capitalistic society, when companies fail, others rise in their place, stronger and more productive. Excesses get flushed out of the market during downturns and only the best and strongest businesses survive. Room is made for new ideas and better business models to replace the old and inefficient. The U.S. always rebounds well from recessions when capitalism is allowed to work.

Can anyone explain to me how moving away from capitalism, where free markets decide winners and losers, is going to help the economy? Aren't all the other growing economies, like China and India, moving toward capitalism to lift their poor out of poverty? Why are we going in the wrong direction?

Sadly, when the virtues of capitalism are not taught in the schools, addressed by the media, or taught by parents to their children in the home, it is not hard to convince people to abandon capitalism in the face of a recession.

One final thought. The end result of socialism is always the same—wealth-creation diminishes, the entrepreneurial spirit is destroyed, and people take on an attitude of "Why work hard and take risks if the government is going to confiscate my wealth?" As a result, there are fewer and fewer well-paying, private-sector jobs available. More and more people are forced to look to the government to employ them and supply their needs. Eventually, many of the go-getters, risk-takers, innovators, and achievers either leave the country or they quit taking risks and investing in the economy. As tax revenues dwindle, the government continues to squeeze the declining wealth created by the private sector, taking more and more private property and assets, and transferring it to people who support the socialist government. Eventually, you have all ambition, freedom, and sense of self-reliance taken from the people by their own power-hungry government. Political corruption increases as it becomes one of the few ways to achieve power and wealth. We can already see this pattern forming in America.

Hopefully, one quick whiff of socialism under President Obama these next four years will disgust Americans back into their good sense. If we can seize the moment by educating Americans on the virtues of capitalism, while offering common-sense solutions to our challenges, conservatives will be able to lead a new generation of Americans to prosperity under the beautiful but imperfect system of capitalism.

★ *Part III* ★

REFORMING OUR INSTITUTIONS

SOLVING OUR EDUCATION CRISIS

Educate and inform the whole mass of the people....They
are the only sure reliance for the preservation of liberty.

—THOMAS JEFFERSON[1]

OUR FOUNDING FATHERS believed that an educated citizenry was crucial to the survival and future well-being of the new nation they were in the process of building. In 1777, in a letter to his son, John Adams wrote that it was vital to teach the next generation about America's founding values and principles if freedom and independence were to be preserved. Seventy years later, Abraham Lincoln also emphasized the link between the quality of education and the nation's welfare: "The philosophy of the school room in one generation will be the philosophy of government in the next."[2]

Since its birth, Americans have placed heavy emphasis on the importance of education. The transformation of a small group of disparate colonies into the most powerful nation on earth—economically, politically, and militarily—is a testament to the talent, skills, knowledge, and innovative character our people developed over the years through our system of education.

Today, we expect our educational system to produce young adults who can read, write, do basic math, have life skills, and compete successfully in the global environment. We should also want our youth to be of good character, hardworking, physically fit, and able to maximize their God-given talents. Americans are willing to pay to achieve these objectives, spending more money on public education than any other nation (with the exception of Switzerland): $9,000 per pupil annually.[3] Despite the high degree of public support and level of investment for our system (which features massive federal involvement and control through the Department of Education and powerful teachers' unions) the results over the past three decades have been terrible.

Our high school graduation rate ranks near the bottom among industrialized democracies in the triennial assessment of student achievement that the Paris-based Organisation for Economic Co-operation and Development (OECD) conducts of its thirty member countries.[4] Recent results are sobering, with the performance of American secondary school students varying from mediocre to poor. In a 2007 study of fifteen-year-old students, the OECD found that the United States ranked in the middle of that organization's thirty member countries in reading literacy, but near the bottom every-where else, placing twenty-first in scientific literacy, twenty-fifth in mathematics literacy, and twenty-fourth in problem-solving.[5]

In a 2007 study of Science Competencies for Tomorrow's World, the OECD drew a number of conclusions about the performance of U.S. high school students. One was that the U.S. has an average number of students who perform at the highest proficiency levels, but a much larger proportion who perform at the lowest levels.[6] The U.S. was the only industrialized nation to have relatively high numbers of both top and bottom performers. The OECD also found significant disparities among various American ethnic groups. While white students' average science score (523) ranked above the average of the thirty countries studied, Hispanic Amer-ican (439), American Indian, Native Alaskan (436), and African American (409) students all fell far below.[7] These groups scored similarly to the national averages of Turkey and Mexico, the two lowest-performing OECD countries. The lesson is clear: our educa-tional system (with stronger support from the families) must do a better job of educating the ethnic minority populations of the nation.

As it is, *each year almost one-third of our high school students are not finishing high school.*[8] The dropout rate is even higher for minorities and students from low-income families. This is not just a problem for these individuals; it is a problem for the communities and the nation. It is estimated that some 75 percent of the crimes in the country are committed by individuals who have not completed high school.[9] Dropouts are also more likely to go on welfare and have higher health costs than high school graduates.[10] They can expect, on average, to earn only about 60 percent of what their graduating peers will earn and about 40 percent of those with college degrees.[11]

If there is any good news, it is that the U.S. continues to have the best university and advanced studies institutions and programs in the world. It should be noted, however, that an inordinately high proportion of our top university students in science, mathematics, economics, the fine arts, and even social sciences are foreign students from Asia and the Near East, or second-generation Americans whose parents came from those regions.[12]

Beyond that, one can question what our universities are teaching, or not teaching. In 2005 the Intercollegiate Studies Institute (ISI) contracted with the University of Connecticut's Department of Public Policy to administer a two-year study of tests of basic historical and civic knowledge to fourteen thousand students at fifty top schools, including Yale, Harvard, Cornell, Duke, Brown, the University of Virginia, and others. For two years, America's elite universities and colleges failed to rise above D-plus on these tests. The average score by the college seniors was 53.2 percent on the civic-literacy test.[13]

The survey also found the following:

1. students were no better off when they left the universities and colleges than when they arrived in terms of acquiring knowledge of civics;
2. an Ivy League education did nothing to contribute to a student's civic learning.[14]

———•◦•———

Another challenge that our colleges and universities are facing today is the assault on free speech. Over the past few years, there has been an alarming increase of efforts by students on the political Left to prevent speakers from presenting opposing conservative views. For example, at the University of North Carolina an eminent guest speaker was driven from the platform by a mob of leftist students and outsiders who did not want to hear or let others hear what he had to say about illegal immigration.[15] Many in the mob had been stirred up and mobilized by the pro-amnesty lobby.

This sorry situation extends to the faculty. Professors with conservative Republican views are being harassed by students who try to organize boycotts of their classes or have them fired by downgrading them in universities and colleges that use student grading of faculty. There have also been substantiated reports of liberal professors in some of our top schools working to deny their conservative colleagues tenure and to prevent applicants who fail to manifest a liberal orthodoxy from gaining employment in the school in the first place.

Beyond that, what can one say about the performance of the faculty of our colleges and universities who stay quiet in the face of the attacks on free speech, and, worse, those who actually condone and support them? Our universities were established as bastions of free speech and are expected to provide our youth with opportunities to hear all sides of the issues. Millions of Americans have fought and died to protect this freedom, yet many of our university administrators and faculty stand silent.

Attacks on free speech have been tried and have been successful in other countries; in Germany, for example, before World War II. Let's call those who would take away our right to free speech and deny our people the opportunity to hear differing points of view what they are: fascists. This incipient fascism that our university system now condones is a threat to democracy and it must be stopped in its tracks right now.

WHAT ARE WE TEACHING?

Clearly, many reforms in our educational system are needed, and urgently. Where do we begin? In my view, we should first revisit what our children are being taught. We should return to our Founding Fathers for wisdom and their belief that our youth must be educated in a manner that prepares them to take over the job of protecting and maintaining our republic and all the values and opportunities it embodies.

Our children must understand how the United States employs freedom, capitalism, a limited federal government, and its people's ingenuity, hard work, and great character to become the world's most powerful and prosperous nation. They should be required to learn the values and principles of our government as set forth in the Declaration of Independence and our Constitution.

For the first 150 years, schools fulfilled this mission. Now, the vast majority of children graduating from public high schools have no clue as to the values of our Founding Fathers, nor have they seriously studied the very short U.S. Constitution or Declaration of Independence. I doubt seriously that many of them could articulate the differences between capitalism, socialism, and communism, or describe the economic system by which America has grown prosperous.

A survey conducted by the Intercollegiate Studies Institute (ISI) proves my point. The ISI gave a random sample of 2,508 Americans a thirty-three-question civics exam, with the average score of 49 percent. Test-takers were given a multiple-choice question concerning the definition of *capitalism*. Only 53 percent answered correctly. About 20 percent said capitalism is a system in which supply and demand are decided by a majority vote, and another 20 percent said they believe it is a system in which the government implements policies that favor businesses over consumers.[16]

Knowing why capitalism creates so much wealth, produces so many opportunities for people, and a high standard of living is incredibly important. How can the wealthiest country in the world fail to teach its children how it became so wealthy? That is about as dumb as it gets. And liberal educators have purposefully failed to teach our children the benefits of capitalism.

Presently, we focus almost all of our attention on students passing standardized tests. Many schools have no choice because this is required to continue to receive federal and state funding. We are not, at the same time, making the necessary effort to produce responsible, well-rounded adults with life skills, ready to compete in today's global economy.

I believe in accountability for our schools, but having schools simply judged based on tests that are so narrowly focused falls far short of what is required if we are to meet our educational goals enumerated earlier. For example, common sense dictates that finance be taught at the lower levels in our education system so that our children have a solid understanding of money, credit, debt, investment, interest, inflation, and bankruptcy as they enter into the marketplace, with all its possible pitfalls. The understanding of these principles should be required in all our standardized testing.

TEACHING THE FOUNDING FATHERS' JUDEO-CHRISTIAN VALUES

One truth and founding principle that unites us as Americans, as declared by the Founders in the Declaration of Independence, is that we have a Creator who cares about us and gives us rights. Now, most of our schools teach evolution exclusively, without even informing our children of this unifying statement in our Declaration of Independence upon which this nation was founded. It is no great surprise that after many years of this false, misleading teaching that so many of our children believe that they have evolved from apes and their lives have no purpose. A wise friend once told me, "If you teach kids they come from monkeys, do not be surprised if they act like monkeys."

For the first 150 years, the U.S. Supreme Court in its opinions on several occasions called America a Christian nation and wrote that the laws of the country were based on biblical values. Does anyone believe that this is taught in our school system? Now, we have a President who flatly declares we are not a Christian nation; this coming from a man who Democrats claim is a constitutional scholar.

One thing is certain: the Founders were willing to die to give themselves, their children, and us a country that reverenced and honored God and the values of the Bible upon which they based our founding documents. They also believed strongly in freedom of religion and that everyone had the God-given right to practice his or her own religion or no religion at all, as long as it caused no harm to another. These are incontrovertible facts about our Founding Fathers that should be taught in every school because these are the reasons we even have this great country, with all its freedoms and privileges. Our public school system, with its largely secular and/or liberal teachers and administrators, teaches our children very differently from our Founders' principles.

CHARACTER-BUILDING EDUCATION

Tragically, too many of our children now grow up in single-parent homes (40 percent of U.S. children are born to unmarried women[17]) or dysfunctional homes, where their hearts and minds are not being properly trained and their character suffers. Moreover, our public schools do not do much, if any, character training. As a result, America is turning out far too few hardworking, motivated young adults with self-esteem and concern for their community and nation.

As a parent of a five-year-old and a seven-year-old, I know first-hand that much of a child's character has already been developed by age seven. We need to make sure we reach these kids very early and let them know they are loved, while teaching and showing them how to love others and respect authority and rules. In Florida, we have a "Learning for Life" character education program that is woefully underfunded, under-publicized, and largely unused. If instituted, from pre-K through twelfth grade, this program, and other character-training programs, would make a tremendous difference in the lives of our children, with spectacular societal consequences. The legislators, school administrators, and public at large, however, do not prioritize such programs.

If we develop our children's character with intensive daily training from pre-K through twelfth grade, then reading, writing, and the desire to learn and stay in school would take care of itself. Currently, many of our kids drop out of school due to boredom, lack of character, and lack of purpose. Continuing to pour more money into our public schools, which have been greatly underperforming as a whole, mostly due to apathetic, unmotivated kids, is crazy. We have been doing that for years now and it is not working.

We can make all the laws we want, but if we do not turn out a society of high character, self-reliant, and well-educated adults, we will not continue for much longer as a prosperous and secure society. If we want our crime rates, drug use, and dependency rates to go down, with more people living productive lives and contributing to their communities, we will invest in character-building education immediately and on a large scale, including experimental pilot programs, some in cities, some in the suburbs, and some in rural areas.

OTHER EDUCATIONAL REFORMS

I strongly believe in school choice, including charter schools, home-schooling, and private schools. I believe in tax credits for parents choosing to opt for such schools to compensate for the taxes they pay for the public schools. Every parent should be able to choose the school of his or her choice. Competition among schools is critical to a successful educational program for our children, particularly in poorer neighborhoods. Certainly, no children should be disadvantaged in any way by being forced into a failing public school system.

For the defenders of the public school system who are opposed to vouchers and school choice, I ask this: is the public school system producing motivated, well-rounded children of good character, who understand our government, basic economics, and are ready to compete for high-paying jobs after all the increased spending our nation has thrown at our schools over the last twenty years? From 2001 to 2006 alone, we have increased federal spending on education by 137 percent,[18] so our failures have not been due to a refusal to spend more money. The answer to this question is obviously no, and wholesale reform is needed, as opposed to dumping more and more money into a failing system.

We must also tackle head-on the loss of U.S. leadership in the fields of science and technology by improving the teaching of science and mathematics at all educational levels, beginning with rigorous courses at both the primary and secondary levels. Newt Gingrich had a great idea. He suggested that we provide scholarships to children at an early age that would allow them to attend the best colleges and grad schools in return for five years of service in a well-paid government job, to specifically encourage scientific achievement.

Successful educational reform will require taking on the teachers union, the National Education Association (NEA), which remains a major impediment to the improvement of education in America. It is almost impossible to fire underperforming teachers as the union invariably steps in to object. The NEA also resists attempts to reward some teachers over others (e.g., to give math and science teachers greater compensation) and often thwarts the introduction of new programs designed to motivate the "best and the brightest."

It goes without saying that ultimately there is no substitute for good parenting. Show me a society where parents do a good job of loving their children and training them to be respectful, hard-working, and motivated to learn, and I will show you well-educated young adults. Conversely, show me a society where parents do not train their children's hearts and minds properly, and I will show you a failed educational system just trying to make the best out of an unworkable situation, as well as a failing society overall.

CHRISTIANS ARISE AND FIGHT FOR AMERICA: THE ROLE OF THE CHURCH

Are you willing to spend time studying the issues, making yourself aware and then conveying that information to family and friends? Will you resist the temptation to get a government handout for your community? Realize that the doctor's fight against socialized medicine is your fight. We can't socialize the doctors without socializing the patients. Recognize that government invasion of public power is eventually an assault upon your own business. If some among you fear taking a stand because you are afraid of reprisals from customers, clients or even government, recognize that you are just feeding the crocodile hoping he'll eat you last.
—RONALD REAGAN, OCTOBER 27, 1964[1]

ANOTHER STRIKING DIFFERENCE between the Founders' times and today lies within the Christian Church. In the Founding Fathers' days, the church, with its many denominations, led the fight for America's independence and the establishment of a good government based on biblical principles. Church leaders understood their responsibility to help lead and steward the new nation. And church members, who constituted the overwhelming majority of people who gave us this nation, were willing to fight and die for a country that promised everyone freedom to practice his own religion.

Clearly, every nation has a value system as the basis of its laws. In Iran, for example, their Sharia law is based on a radical form of the Islamic religion. In Afghanistan, women who are raped are punished as though they were the criminals. In other countries, laws are simply created to suit a dictator's whims and not based on the citizens' set of beliefs or any particular religious values.

From the start, America was different. Our Founders did not want to be subject to an arbitrary belief system of a dictator or a centralized government. Those who formed our nation based the laws on Judeo-Christian values contained in the Bible. This made sense, since the great majority of our first citizens were Christians. America has since operated as a Christian nation with laws based on biblical values.

In 1892, in *Church of the Holy Trinity v. United States*, the Supreme Court stated, "No purpose of action against religion can be imputed to any legislation, State or national, because this is a religious people... This is a Christian nation."[2] The Court declared that, "Christianity, general Christianity, is, and always has been, a part of the common law... not Christianity with an established church... but Christianity with liberty of conscience to all men."[3] In 1931, in *U.S. v. Macintosh*, the Supreme Court reiterated that, "We are a Christian people, according to one another the equal right of religious freedom and acknowledging with reverence the duty of obedience to the will of God."[4]

In nearly eighty years, however, our institutions, including the Supreme Court, the media, and our educational system, have successfully removed the fact that we are a Christian nation, with Christian values and laws, from the public consciousness. In 1947, in *Everson v. Board of Education*, the Supreme Court suddenly announced, "The First Amendment has erected a wall between church and state."[5] Following this declaration, the courts have been striking down religious Christian expression and activity, which had heretofore been constitutional.

Since that fateful Supreme Court decision, the church and too many of its members have allowed America to forget its Christian heritage and associated values without much of a fight. As a result, we are quickly becoming a nation with no moral compass. The definition of marriage is under attack; nearly half of marriages end in divorce[6]; out-of-wedlock births have risen from 18 percent to 40 percent since 1980[7]; children are growing up without fathers in their homes; crime and drug use are out of control; fraud and corruption are rampant on Wall Street *and* in government; there is no respect for the rule of law (see Chapter 19, "Ending Illegal Immigration"); and our politicians routinely ignore the Constitution they are sworn to uphold. When the church does engage politically, it typically fights for social issues such as traditional marriage, the sanctity of life, and school prayer. These are extremely important battles to be fought and many Christian leaders have done a great job with too little support from the church as a whole. On other critical issues, the church has neglected to even take a stand. For example, there has been a complete failure by the church to fulfill its role in fighting for balanced budgets, which future generations have a right to expect.

Most church leaders also have displayed an unwillingness to fight for, and speak out about, the principles of the Founding Fathers and our Constitution. The church should demand these truths be taught to our children in both Christian and public schools. As Christians, our church has a responsibility to make sure its members are acutely aware of the nation's roots and founding documents, are politically informed, and excellent stewards of the nation.

Finally, Christians are responsible to seek God's wisdom on godly stewardship principles in financial issues, as well. We owe it to our nation and our children to understand how wealth is created, how to manage it properly, and what economic system best lifts people out of poverty and helps people reach their God-given potential.

We are commanded by God to tend to the orphans and widows, the poor and afflicted, and we all should do our very best to minister to them. The Bible never suggests, however, that government set up big welfare programs, tax job creators heavily, or that people should look to the government as the source of their blessings and provision. In fact, it states something far different.

The role of churches, synagogues, charities, non-profits, and private citizens, is to help those in need. They do a much better job of administering aid than the government. This is because these organizations, and the people associated with them, truly care about the people they are helping. They also have natural incentives to be efficient with their money and make sure the people that receive help are also working hard to help themselves or the help will stop. Contrast this with the attitude and capacity of "Big Government" to carry out this important work exemplified by its pitiful response to Hurricane Katrina.

When compassion is freely given, there are two big winners: the recipient and the giver. When money is simply forcibly taken from people by the government to redistribute wealth, no one profits, no one is blessed, and the nation's soul decays. People need to be encouraged to work hard, not to complain about a lack of government benefits. The government is not and was never intended to be the provider of individual needs. The church should be the venue for teaching this principle.

The church has been too silent on corruption in government and has made virtually no attempt to help break up the abusive power of the career-politician Congress. Church members are too often politically uninformed and unmotivated and have voted into federal, state, and local offices some of our worst, most corrupt politicians. Church leaders and members must be active in procuring a moral and effective government, while it helps to promote great leaders that its members actively support. If they fail, this nation is likely to continue to be ruled by special interest-financed politicians who are destroying our great nation.

If the church does not want to lead, I assure you there are many secular, power-hungry people who are already working hard to advance their agenda. It is also clear, from observing our institutions like education, Congress, the media, the presidency, and the U.S. Supreme Court, who is winning this fight. There is a saying in politics that the most passionate side wins. We Christians had better do some serious soul-searching to find out what we are made of and whether we are willing to rise to our duty. As David said before his epic fight with Goliath, "Is there not a cause?" (1 Sam. 17:29).

THE U.S. SUPREME COURT'S LEADING ROLE IN AMERICA'S DECLINE

I do not forget the position assumed by some that Constitutional questions are to be decided by the Supreme Court....At the same time, the candid citizen must confess that if the policy of the government upon vital questions affecting the whole people is to be irrevocably fixed by decisions of the Supreme Court, the instant they are made...the people will have ceased to be their own rulers, having resigned their government into the hands of that eminent tribunal.
—ABRAHAM LINCOLN, FIRST INAUGURAL, MARCH 4, 1861[1]

WHEN GEORGE WASHINGTON selected the members to the first Supreme Court in 1789, he used seven criteria, with the degree of their support and advocacy for the Constitution at the very top of his list. Over the decades that have followed, the Court has been variously described as the Constitution's "voice," its "defender," and its "guardian." Over those decades, however, the Supreme Court has strayed from the limited but powerful role that its creators had envisioned and began blurring the lines between supporting and advocating constitutional principles and legislating via a judicial activism mentality. President Lincoln's fear has come true.

We have recent examples of the effect of this changing role of the Court: its failure to contain the expansion of federal powers; its complicity in the Congress's expansive tax-and-spend policies; the *Roe v. Wade* decision on abortion; and its central role in the removal of Christian values from the nation's institutions.

STATES' RIGHTS AND LIMITED GOVERNMENT

Our Founding Fathers were particularly concerned about the abuse of centralized power, having just suffered from it under Great Britain. The doctrine of states' rights was first discussed at the Constitutional Convention of 1787 and advanced by Thomas Jefferson in 1798. The Founders made it very clear in the Constitution and in the Bill of Rights that the federal government would have very limited power in the United States, with most power reserved for the states and the people.

Over the years, however, this doctrine has been watered down and neglected by the Supreme Court, especially at times of a "perfect storm," when a more liberal Court has intersected a liberal executive branch and a liberal Congress. In particular, after Franklin D. Roosevelt's election in 1932, federal powers were extended far beyond those expressly granted to the federal government under the Constitution, with activist Court justices stretching the limits even of what is "implied" under the Constitution, let alone expressly stated.

The result is today's "nanny state," with a federal hand in almost every aspect of the lives of the citizens. This, of course, is nirvana for collectivists and career politicians in Congress and their constituents. And, unfortunately, this is the desire of too many Americans who have grown up looking to Washington, D.C., for handouts.

The transfer of resources is astounding. Over the past two decades, government spending has grown nearly four times faster than our national economy.[2] In 2008, the federal government spent $2.9 trillion,[3] almost 21 percent of the country's total economy.[4] The size of the bureaucracy required to manage this largesse has, not surprisingly, grown apace. Whereas there were only a few hundred government employees two centuries ago, today there are nearly 2.8 million.[5]

Most important, critical decisions in the lives of our citizens, well beyond taxation and expenditures that should be made at the state and local levels, are now made in Washington. They include issues involving almost every aspect of daily living, including education, religion, health, business, and management of our environment and natural resources. In the process, individual liberties that the Founding Fathers wished to protect at all costs are being narrowed and constrained, little by little, federal law by federal law. In his book *Conscience of a Conservative*, Barry Goldwater observed that the Constitution is now treated as a kind of political handbook in political theory, to be heeded or ignored depending on how it fits the plans of contemporary officials.[6]

How did our national government grow from a servant with sharply limited powers into a master with unlimited power? Partly, we have been swindled by politicians who promised to restore limited government, but then, after the election, expanded government's role. Mostly, however, it has not been the broken promises, but the kept promises that have been destroying our freedom. We keep electing politicians who tell us what we can have for "free" if they are elected.

You may be shocked to learn that your Congress has no constitutional authority to spend money on earmarks for teapot museums, bridges to nowhere, or local projects. It has no authority to bail out individual banks or automakers, as those expenditures are certainly not for the "general welfare" authorized by the Constitution, but only to benefit local interests or a very small part of the population affected. There is certainly no constitutional authority for Congress to spend taxpayer dollars collected from all fifty states to help pay for California's $500 billion debt or other states' debts because these states are spending more money than they are willing to collect from their residents. Amazingly, this issue is rarely discussed by our media or our congressional representatives.

Let's examine how and why our Congress is acting outside of its constitutional authority. The federal government's only authority in the Constitution for collecting taxes and spending taxpayer's money is found in Article 1, Section 8: "The Congress shall have power to lay and collect taxes, duties, imposts and excises, to pay the debts and provide for the common defense and general welfare of the United States."[7] This precedes a list of specific items for which the Congress has spending authority such as to "raise and support Armies, provide and maintain a Navy and establish Post Offices and post Roads."[8] Moreover, the Tenth Amendment to the Constitution states, "The powers not delegated to the United States by the Constitution, nor prohibited by it to the States, are reserved to the States respectively, or to the people."[9]

Some of the Founders who were most passionate about states' rights, like Thomas Jefferson and James Madison, argued that the Taxing and Spending Clause ("common defense and general welfare" language) conferred on Congress no additional power whatsoever, that it was merely a summary or general description of the specific items, which followed immediately thereafter. Others, like Alexander Hamilton, believed Congress was given authority to spend on other "general welfare" items not specifically listed in the Constitution. No one, including Hamilton, argued or believed Congress was given the power to spend for needs of a state, community, or for an individual business.

In 1936, the Supreme Court in *United States v. Butler* accepted Hamilton's more liberal interpretation. But Justice Owen Roberts made it clear that "The powers of taxation and appropriation *extend only* to matters of national, as distinguished from local, welfare" (emphasis mine).[10] The U.S. Supreme Court, of course, would determine what constitutes general welfare.

So, how did we get to the point of our federal government bankrupting the nation by spending hundreds of billions on local projects and individual corporate and state bailouts? Less than a year after *United States v. Butler*, the Court abandoned its opinion in *Butler* in the *Helvering v. Davis* case. The Court held that although Congress was limited by the Constitution to spend only for the "general welfare," members of Congress could decide for themselves what constitutes the general welfare. But—*no taxing and spending bill from Congress has since then ever been invalidated because it did not serve the general welfare.*[11] The primary reason in any such example has been that the U.S. Supreme Court has repeatedly denied any taxpayer attempt to challenge congressional spending as being unconstitutional, holding that the taxpayer has not suffered injury and, therefore, has no standing to bring such lawsuit. Your Congress is aware the Supreme Court bars such lawsuits and because career politicians love bringing pork project money back to their districts and states, this unconstitutional practice continues year after year.

Under the Supreme Court's interpretation, money for earmarks for local purposes, like a teapot museum, is constitutional. On the other hand, when a presidential line-item veto law to get rid of these unconstitutional spending projects was passed into law with strong popular support, the Court ruled this to be unconstitutional. This is utterly inexplicable.

We obviously are not living in a country whose federal government respects and honors the Constitution. We, in fact, now reside in a nation in which nine unelected U.S. Supreme Court justices and the legislative branch collude to do as they please. Most of our justices consider themselves the great arbitrator of right and wrong. They refer to the Constitution as a "living document," which is code for "we can stretch it, ignore it, and twist it" in whatever expedient way we want to. They deem their intellect far superior to the language of this old, outdated document that can be a nice guide on occasion. As Reagan told us, concentrated power is always bad!

I watch, read, and listen to politics almost every day. I cannot recall the last time I heard any President or Congressman argue that while a certain spending program might have a legitimate purpose, unfortunately our hands are tied because we are limited by the Constitution and the Tenth Amendment as to our authority and power and that this is an area reserved to states and local governments. I think I have not heard such a sentiment since President Reagan in the eighties.

Unless the public is willing to fight for its return as the law of the land, which I pray they will, we really should have a formal burial for the Tenth Amendment. It clearly is dead and there is no sense pretending it has any meaning to our federal government. The Tenth Amendment at least deserves a ceremony honoring all of its accomplishments and greatness in helping form the freest, most prosperous nation on earth for 230 years!

We are actually living under a President, Congress, and Supreme Court who read the Constitution as if it says:

> Congress shall have unlimited power to collect taxes and spend taxpayer dollars for any reason it desires. There are no limits on this power. It can tax and spend for the general welfare, a corporation's welfare, a special-interest group's welfare, or to transfer money to individual cities, counties, or states. It can use this tax-and-spend power to redistribute income according to its desire. It can also use this unlimited power to borrow trillions from future generations.
>
> The individuals and states shall be powerless to strip the federal government of any of this power. Taxpayers have no standing to bring a suit against Congress under this Constitution. This tax-and-spend power was not given to this government by God or by the expressed desire of the people but was conferred upon it by the federal government's own desires. Hence, the federal government shall do as it pleases.

More evidence to suggest the "Conservative Comeback" is underway can be found in the recent news that several states (including Alaska, Idaho, Oklahoma, and both Dakotas) have recently passed state sovereignty (Tenth Amendment) laws warning the federal government to "cease and desist" from interfering unlawfully with their affairs.[12] Many other states are following suit. In addition, a popular new Web site, tenthamendmentcenter.com, is attracting twenty thousand new visitors every day. Maybe we will not have to have our burial ceremony for the Tenth Amendment after all!

ABORTION AND *ROE V. WADE*

One of the saddest aspects of the decline in American values has been the increase in the number of abortions over the last fifty years. This is despite the fact that virtually all Americans agree that reducing abortions in the country is a laudable goal.

The floodgates opened in 1973 with the Supreme Court's *Roe v. Wade* decision, which legalized abortions in the U.S. In my view, this was one of the most indefensible decisions ever rendered by our Supreme Court as a matter of law. As a lawyer who has read the Constitution many times, I can safely say there is simply no constitutional right to an abortion. I invite everyone to read the Constitution and then show me where a women's right to choose to abort a baby is addressed. Abortion rights are not discussed, nor is there even a "right to privacy" clause in the Constitution on which such rights according to the Supreme Court are based.

To the contrary, the Constitution and the Declaration of Independence requires the Court to protect life, not legalize its destruction. Liberal judges just simply substituted their own opinions and made up law to achieve their desired result. Nowhere in the Constitution does it say that a woman's rights and the fetuses' rights change in the various trimesters. Yet, that is what the U.S. Supreme Court, in "interpreting the Constitution," claims it says. If that is a true and correct interpretation of the Constitution, we might as well not even have a Constitution anymore because our justices in the highest court of the land can interpret it in any ridiculous manner they choose.

In fact, a better argument can be made that an unborn child *is* life and should be constitutionally protected. I know this much: every life is expected to receive equal protection under our Constitution. Not only did the Court not protect these lives, but it then went further and said that states do not have the right to protect these lives, either. In effect, it decreed that the Court is the great decider on this matter and has the authority to decide when life begins, not the people.

As a Christian living in a country founded on Christian principles, it is difficult to accept nine appointed, unelected judges making such a decision. When this subject arises, I recall what the Bible says about God and His creations:

> You made all the delicate, inner parts of my body and knit me together in my mother's womb. Thank you for making me so wonderfully complex! Your workmanship is marvelous—how well I know it. You watched me as I was being formed in utter seclusion, as I was woven together in the dark of the womb. You saw me before I was born. Every day of my life was recorded in your book. Every moment was laid out before a single day had passed.
>
> —PSALM 139:13–16, NLT

Having said this about *Roe v. Wade*, the real challenge for us all is to turn the hearts of people against abortion. It is much more important to change hearts and minds than it is to change laws. We have laws against illegal immigration, but nobody follows those. We need to get to the point where more and more Americans are adamantly opposed to abortion. Only then will abortion rates decrease significantly with or without any change in the law.

How do we accomplish this goal? I know being angry or judgmental against people who believe differently is not the way. We should be teaching and educating our youth and instilling biblical values while passionately fighting for laws that will be effective in deterring abortions.

I believe that one of the most powerful ways for abortions to begin to be utilized less often as an option for women would be the passage of ultrasound bills at the state level. While they preserve a woman's right to choose, ultrasounds can be a powerful force for reducing the number of abortions in our country

These bills have already passed in many states. In Florida, former State Senator Daniel Webster introduced a bill in 2007 requiring women be provided an opportunity to view an ultrasound in the first trimester before making a decision to abort the fetus. Women would thus have accurate and complete information and greater appreciation of what they were destroying before making an irreversible life-and-death decision. If women viewed these ultrasounds at ten or twelve weeks, they would see fingers and toes forming and realize just how developed their baby already is at this early stage. For many, this shocking reality would cause them to be affected enough to choose to keep their child. Information and truth is critical when making a decision affecting the baby and both parents. I believe fighting for the ultrasound bills at the state level should be one of the great goals of the church and of all people who care about the protection of life.

THE CONSTITUTION AND RELIGION IN OUR SCHOOLS

The Founding Fathers placed strong emphasis on a central role for religion in American life. They were mindful that the country was settled by people fleeing religious persecution in other lands and also of the important role that religion would play in building a moral and ethical nation. The large majority of the Founders were practicing Christians and many believed that Bible teaching had an important place in the schools. They further agreed that what was taught, and how, was a role properly reserved for each state.

If the Founders had desired to keep religion out of state schools or did not want Bible-teaching in any of their schools, they would have said so in the Constitution and thus overridden any prerogatives that the states and individuals might have claimed. Nowhere in the Constitution is the Supreme Court given the authority to decide these issues.

There are only two references to religion in the Constitution. The first one is found in Article 6: "No religious test shall ever be required as a qualification for any office or public trust under the United States."[13] The second one is found in the First Amendment to the Constitution: "Congress shall make no law respecting an establishment of religion, or prohibiting the free exercise thereof."[14]

In recent decades, the Supreme Court has addressed a wide variety of issues related to the role of religion in American society, including its lawful place in both our public and private institutions and the school system. Consistently, the Court has whittled away and narrowed the responsibility of the states for controlling the operation of the public schools, what our educational institutions may teach, and has taken away the people's right to decide.

In 1947, the Court held Bible teaching in schools unconstitutional. Since then, symbols and references that have been longstanding and cherished parts of the American culture have come under attack. These include the "In God We Trust" motto on our coins, Christmas greetings and ornament displays, and the reference to "under God" in the *Pledge of Allegiance* and school prayers, even if they are non-sectarian.

There is a tremendous book entitled *Original Intent*, written by David Barton, that details how the U.S. Supreme Court has taken God out of our country, decision-by-decision, and I encourage all of you to read it.[15]

As we look to the future, and to the highest court in the land as our protector and defender of the Constitution, there is very little in the recent performance of the Supreme Court to inspire hope in the tens of millions of us who love our "one nation under God." It would take a dramatic shift and election of new justices to return the Court to a limited institution, which protects the Constitution and the values of our Founders. President Obama's choice of Sonia Sotomayor will probably not be the answer to our prayers.

Dismantling Congress's Incumbency Protection Program

Concentrated power has always been the enemy of liberty.
—Ronald Reagan[1]

OUR CONGRESS IS often described these days as being dysfunctional. This criticism is not entirely justified. It does function rather well—for the Congressmen and Congresswomen! Much of the structure and workings of the Congress are relics of the past. The vast majority of Americans agree that the system is broken and does not work to help solve our national challenges. Nevertheless, it remains that way because it is in the interest of the incumbents to keep the status quo and the odds are heavily stacked against those who would try to reform it.

At the heart of the problem is that the system has created a very comfortable lifestyle with celebrity status and much power to a few career politicians. Ronald Reagan observed:

> The one thing our Founding Fathers could not foresee...was a nation governed by professional politicians who had an interest in getting re-elected. They probably envisioned a fellow serving a couple of hitches and then eagerly looking forward to getting back to the farm.[2]

The length of tenure of members of Congress is astounding and depressing. As of 2010, Robert Byrd has roamed the halls for fifty-eight years! John Dingell is running close behind at fifty-five years. Then we have Daniel Inouye, fifty-one years; John Conyers, forty-five years; David Obey, forty-one years; and Bill Young, Thad

Cochran, Pete Stark, and Don Young, all with nearly forty years in the institution. How can they really understand the conditions and needs of their constituents when they have led such insular lives, pampered by staff, puffed up with power, showered with accolades and perks from throngs of lobbyists, and set up for life with great entitlement benefits? The answer is, they can't. Moreover, their refusal to voluntarily give up their power says a lot about their sense of self-importance and self-concern at the expense of our country and its 300-plus million citizens. Contrast the values of our present-day Congress with those of George Washington, who walked away from the presidency after two terms due to his strong belief in disbursed power and a government by and for the people.

One of the worst aspects of the career-politician situation is the seniority system. What sets the above-named long-termers apart from their younger counterparts in the House and Senate is the seniority system, which is the basis for awarding committee assignments. None of these top leadership positions is awarded based on accomplishment but is given based on congressional longevity to many of the most self-serving, out-of-touch, special-interest-bought career politicians in our nation's history. No wonder we have a $12-plus trillion debt, many billions a year wasted due to Medicare fraud, and no energy policy!

Any attempt to reorganize the Congress to achieve greater efficiency and cost-savings is invariably met with howls of outrage from any chairman whose committee's jurisdiction, activities, or spending is called into question. Also, when Congress hands out its largesse through earmarks, for example, it is striking that the districts in which committee chairmen and other longer-lived members reside invariably receive the largest share of the funds. Now, why do you suppose this happens? Merely coincidence...that must be it.

One of the most egregious shortcomings of the present system is that Congress and the American people are denied the fresh ideas and other intellectual contributions that younger, fresher faces would provide. This must change. We need to introduce an "out with the old, in with the new" approach, which, among other merits, would reduce the impact of lobbyists on the political process, a process tainted by the close, mutually rewarding relationships that grow up over the years as congressional members and the lobbyists get to know and understand each others' needs just too well.

Let's consider those folks who work so hard to get us the legislation that they, pardon me, that *we* need—the lobbyists.

In 1968, there were sixty-two registered lobbyists in Washington. By the mid eighties, their number had swelled to some eight thousand, many representing foreign governments. Today, the army of lobbyists has reached almost sixteen thousand even after the recession decreased their numbers somewhat, but still comfortably outnumbering our Congressmen plus their staffs.[3] Between 1998 and 2004, lobbyists spread around at least $13 billion to influence legislation.[4] This cozy relationship seems to have no end; more than three hundred former members of Congress have become lobbyists.[5] The "revolving door" is as much a cottage industry as it is a way of life.

Once again, I wonder for whom those sixty thousand wonderful pages of I.R.S. tax code rules and regulations is working. I wonder who benefits from it being so complex, with so many favors, loopholes, and exceptions. It cannot possibly be the Congressmen and lobbyists—do you think?

The close relationships that are built up over the years between the lawmakers and the lobbying industry have a corrupting influence. The price of admittance for drafting our laws seems to be hundreds of thousands of dollars in campaign contributions, luxurious gifts, and exotic trips for our elected officials. Members of Congress look upon these "gifts" not as bribes to do the bidding of corporate and special interests, but as perks appropriate to their lofty positions of power.

We will never be able to take money out of politics, which gives the incumbents and wealthiest Americans a ridiculous advantage over ordinary citizens to serve and lead the country. Therefore, we need to change the job description and tenure to eliminate the perks, power, and special privileges. That way, we can get people who are there for the right reason: to help solve problems.

The unhappy list goes on of how the system is rigged for the benefit of the career politician at the expense of the American citizen. Most of the congressional districts have, over the years, had their boundaries redrawn (gerrymandered) to protect the Democrat or Republican incumbents. Efforts to reverse this, with the goal of having competitive races, are fought tooth and nail by both parties. Not surprisingly, many congressional races are basically uncontested each year. Since 1980, more than 90 percent of the 435 members of the House of Representatives have won re-election every cycle.[6]

In my congressional district, in and around Orlando, Florida, there are approximately 450,000 possible voters. While many vote in general elections, especially during presidential years, only 15 to 18 percent of registered voters go to the polls for each party's primary election.[7] Since so very few citizens are bothering to vote in primaries and most districts are drawn so they are not competitive between the parties, most incumbents need to keep only about one out of ten voters in their own party happy in order to get re-elected.

Another massive advantage for the incumbents is that the state legislators, the parties, and the special-interest groups virtually always line up to support the incumbent. They know, statistically, that the incumbent almost always wins and they want to be on their good side, for their own self-interest. The media then puts the final nails in the challenger's coffin by first proclaiming that no candidate has a chance unless they have raised a large sum of special-interest money and then barely cover the issues and candidates' solutions in the campaign.

The unwillingness of the American people to support regular folks as they run against the incumbents in their own party's primaries has discouraged bright, problem-solving leaders with great character from running against the career politicians. Few individuals want to suffer the personal attacks from these incumbents and their special-interest groups and devote several years of their life to running a campaign when the public will not get rid of their "powerful" Congressman, no matter what the record. Sadly, voter disgust with the incumbents and politicians translates into people not voting instead of voting to throw the bums out!

The voter apathy now pervasive in this country is a serious threat to the future of our great republic. We fail to rectify this situation at our peril. For these and other reasons, we absolutely must fight for term limits for Congress and, ideally, a Term-Limit Amendment to the Constitution, similar to the two-term limit for president.

I firmly believe that U.S. Senators should be limited to two six-year terms in office and our House of Representatives members to no more than three four-year terms. Thus, no member of either house would serve more than twelve years. On the House side, this would eliminate the current two-year term, which is both unnecessarily costly and time-consuming for our representatives. By the time new members of the House get settled in, they immediately begin to raise money for their next campaign. The fact is that when they are on the job, they spend much of their time worrying about how to repay the large campaign contributors who put them in office and raise the money for re-election. It is no accident that our Congress does such a poor job managing the nation's affairs.

The Founding Fathers had established a two-year cycle for the House members so it would be possible to attract good people willing to leave their farms and serve the country. The job back then did not come with all of the present-day power and benefits, and the incumbents were usually all too anxious to return home after two years. Now, no one ever wants to leave, since he or she has so many privileges. In the unlikely event that any incumbent loses his seat or a member leaves for other reasons, all is not lost. They usually end up making millions of dollars as lobbyists for special-interest groups. As many have observed about Congress, "It's Hollywood for ugly people."

Bringing about the magnitude of change required to remedy this situation is a tall order. It will necessitate an amendment to our Constitution driven by a massive grassroots effort at the state level. Change is possible as demonstrated by the successful term-limits legislation enacted at the state level.

In the interim, candidates in races for the Senate and the House should be routinely pressed by their constituents to sign term-limits pledges. Constituents should then vote against anyone who refuses. We are the party of our Founders, which strongly believes in decentralized power and a limited federal government... aren't we?

At the same time, we should systematically vote out of office all incumbents who have served twelve years, as a matter of principle. In the Republican Party, we should ensure that every incumbent who has served twelve years has a strong conservative opponent who will sign a term-limits pledge and then fight particularly hard to see that a new face is elected. Some fellow conservatives worry that self-imposed term limits on the Republicans would just give liberals more power, but I strongly disagree. I believe that this commitment to decentralized power and selfless leadership would be an act of vision and leadership that the electorate will reward. It will not be difficult for our leaders to mentor bright, young statesmen to replace them. Mentorship is a great mark of effective leadership and we must be led by statesmen, not career politicians, if we are going to turn this country back in the right direction.

One other area that cries out for reform is congressional earmarks, the direction of taxpayer dollars to local projects, usually in the incumbent's home district. Most are found buried in voluminous legislation that few Congressmen (other than the perpetrators) and hardly any citizens have the opportunity or the time to read.

I gave credit to President Obama during the campaign for standing tall with John McCain on the evils of earmarks. But soon after taking office, Obama signed a $410 billion spending bill for 2009 that contained more than 8,500 earmarks![8] Then, to compound this betrayal, both the president and Democratic leaders in Congress actually defended this as progress just because the number of earmarks was down from the previous two years.

Congressmen routinely stuff and hide locally focused "pork" projects into big spending bills, while the beneficiaries reciprocate by raising millions of dollars to fund re-election campaigns. In 1987, President Reagan vetoed a highway bill because it had 152 earmarks.[9] In 2005, a Republican Congress passed a highway bill with 6,371 special projects, costing the taxpayers $24 billion.[10] Those and other earmarks passed by the Republican Congress and President Bush included $50 million for an indoor rainforest, $350,000 for an Inner Harmony Foundation and Wellness Center,[11] and the now-infamous $223 million "Bridge to Nowhere" in Alaska.[12]

David Obey, a Democrat from Wisconsin and chairman of the House Budget Committee, made an interesting argument in support of earmarks by the Congress. During a debate on the floor of the House, he said that he would rather have projects selected by members of Congress than by non-elected bureaucrats in Executive Branch departments and agencies. When I heard this, three thoughts sprang to mind: what about our Constitution that prevents federal spending on local projects? The second was, taxpayer money from Florida is not supposed to be going for local projects in other states like West Virginia, simply because they have ninety-one year old Senator Byrd on appropriations. And the third was, why not have the states and localities fund their own needs since the federal government is nearly $12 trillion in debt? Then we have Maxine Waters, House Democrat from California, answering a question on MSNBC on how she and her colleagues could not have read and digested what was in the 440-page 2009 spending bill with all its earmarks when they had only twenty-four hours to review it. While admitting that she had not been able to read it, she did say that she relies on her staff to review such legislation and to tell her what it is necessary that she know. Do we really want our elected officials voting on complex, pork-laden bills that they have not read? And who exactly are these unelected staffers who have been given so much authority and freedom? The fact is that many of these senior staffers have been around Washington for many years, accumulating considerable power they are not shy about using.

It appears fairly obvious that the system is purposely designed that way to keep the American public in the dark and incumbents re-elected. As we begin the reform of our Congress, stopping this practice of earmarks deserves especially high priority. We should also demand that no spending bill be brought to the floor for a vote until members and the public have had a sufficient time to review it; seven days, at a minimum. It is a travesty and an insult to the American public when Congress takes nine months to draft a $410 billion spending bill and then claims that it must be rammed through within twenty-four hours!

I hope and pray that conservative Republicans in the Congress will take the lead in pushing for these needed reforms. I hope they will encourage and mentor younger people to run for Congress and thus help provide our nation with a continuing flow of new ideas and creative solutions to the great challenges of our day. This was the vision that our Founding Fathers had of service to the country and why George Washington nobly gave up the presidency and all the trappings of power that went with it, for the good of the nation. We sorely need such statesmanship in the halls of Congress.

THE MEDIA: LOSING ITS WAY

*Our liberty depends on the freedom of the press, and
that cannot be limited without being lost.*
—THOMAS JEFFERSON, JANUARY 1786[1]

OUR FOUNDING FATHERS strongly believed that a "free press" was vital to the health, and indeed to the very survival, of the nation that they hoped to build. They viewed the press as having two primary responsibilities: helping to educate the citizens of the new nation; and holding the government accountable to the public for its actions. Today, of course, things are vastly different, as providing entertainment to the masses seems to be our media's preoccupation.

After being enshrined in the Constitution's Bill of Rights, "freedom of the press" has been vigorously defended and protected by our courts and by all political parties over the duration of the nation's existence. Clearly, our republic's well being depends upon an informed public. As citizens, we need unbiased news from a free and independent press to help ensure that our freedom and rights are protected from an overreaching government, while also promoting intelligent, informed votes for our elected leaders, especially our president.

Of course, since the Founding Father's time, one of the greatest changes in American society is the scale and pace at which we citizens receive news and information. In those early years, news traveled at the speed a horse could run, or a ship could sail. If one received a single newspaper a week, or a letter a month, one could consider himself to be well-informed. Today, thanks to television, the Internet, I-Pods, the Blogosphere, and Twitter, we Americans live in an age of constant, instantaneous communication. In 2010, obtaining information is the easy part—the difficult part is judging the reliability and objectivity, importance, and value to society.

In recent years there have been numerous reviews, analyses, and polls carried out on the performance of the media in this country, and the views are consistent, and alarming. Public confidence in our Fourth Estate is at an all-time low, and still slipping. The shortcomings most often cited are inaccurate reporting, sensationalism, trivialization of key issues, poor coverage of important events, the media's short attention span, and the erosion of standards of decency. Some of these came together to form a "perfect storm" of incompetence during the presidential debates last year. The moderators consistently asked questions that did not require the candidates to provide specific solutions to our nation's challenges. I would think that would be the goal. On the few occasions when specific questions were asked about critical national issues, non-responses were invariably offered up by the candidates with no follow-up questions.

I watched almost all of the presidential debates last year and never heard one candidate explain how we are going to pay for our entitlement programs as our elderly population doubles in the next twenty years, or for the new spending programs they were proposing, for that matter. In the ten-plus Democrat debates, not one question was asked about how our national commitment to the rule of law squares with our unwillingness to crack down on illegal immigration or why taxpayers should be forced to work extra hours each week to pay for illegals' health care and other benefits. And, the fact that, in most cases, the politicians were only given a minute to respond on a major topic made no one happy; that is, with the exception of the candidates. As a result, debate listeners and viewers were left with only vague commentary on the issues, and regurgitations of all the ailments of the nation, with very little in the way of insights into how the candidates would actually go about solving the problems or how they would pay for programs they were promoting.

My suggestion for improving the debates is to extend the time provided for answering the questions. They should also restrict the candidates to presenting their principles and specific solutions to each issue. Obviously, in the drawn-out campaign season, we all pretty much know what the major issues are; we do not benefit in any way from the candidates' charade of taking time to regale us with personal tales of woe told to them on the campaign trail or reciting what America's challenges are as part of their brief answer.

If Conservatives were asked today to characterize the media today, most would probably give a one-word response: "biased." The nation's major newspapers like the *New York Times* and major TV networks like NBC, CBS, ABC, and CNN appear to many of us as nothing more then President Obama's cheerleaders who despise the Founders' values and are determined to transform this nation into a secular, socialist European-styled country. All pretense of objectivity has disappeared and more and more conservatives have been forced to flee the old-line media to get their news from Fox, conservative talk shows, or *Drudge Report* on the Internet.

Beyond politics, a major concern with the media lies in the fact that a smaller and smaller number of large corporations control the flow of information and news from TV and newspapers to the American people. In addition to reducing the range of opinion that we are receiving, the quality of what is being reported is highly endangered. Over the past decade, big media has slashed budgets, eviscerated newsrooms, and closed foreign bureaus. News outlets across the country have replaced real reporting with celebrity gossip and the "most interesting murder of the day."

Instead of fulfilling their obligation to inform the public with important news and challenge politician's statements and actions, the massive conglomerates are content to offer up junk news with mindless commentary and murder mysteries because they are cheap to produce. In contrast to earlier times, the big producers today see and treat journalism only as a business, not a public service. The result is that the public becomes less informed each passing year on the critical issues the nation confronts.

As the quality and content of the information has degraded in the print media, and subscribers and advertisers move away to electronic means, the financial impact has caused newspapers and magazines to reduce coverage and staff in a continuing downward spiral. Throw into the mix the millions of bloggers with no journalistic training, literary skills, or real knowledge, and we are all being subjected to a blizzard of information of dubious quality. The news anchors of decades past must be spinning in their graves considering the evening news on most of our for-profit national networks. One must be alert to get the brief glimpse they provide of critical national and international issues before the networks move on to give the audience their requisite daily fix of news of celebrity divorces, sexual misconduct by politicians, and the murder case of the month, issues they cover 24/7 for a short period before dropping them suddenly and completely to move on to some other sensational story.

Of course, journalists and TV reporters play up and dwell on stories that are sensational because they think (and unfortunately know) that this is what sells. I say "unfortunately" because this lust for violence, sex, and scandal on the part of the American public is spreading like a cancer within our society. Just where are we headed with this? The moral fabric of our society is in a race to the bottom, stripped away bit-by-bit, year-by-year with tremendous damage being done to our children and society as a whole.

I am personally not yet ready to throw in the towel. There are measures that the public can take to fight back. And I believe that they are integral to the "Conservative Comeback." For starters, our churches, community groups, and families need to become engaged in the dialogue. Again, it is important to remember Reagan's instruction to us that "All great change takes place at the dinner table."[2] If we want our media to change, we need to come together and demand change, and this process has already begun.

One effective way to bring about change is for conservatives to no longer support advertisers of NBC, CNN, MSNBC, networks that are biased not only in favor of the liberal agenda, but whose on-air commentators, such as MSNBC's Keith Olbermann, are filled with contempt for our Founders' beliefs and each night mislead the American people.

The American Family Association (AFA) does a great job of sending e-mails to let people know which advertisers are supporting which leftist groups. I had a friend recently tell me that he and his colleagues were putting together a Web site to disseminate this type of information. It is incumbent on all of us to find out which corporations are supporting the Left and which businesses are supporting Fox and the conservative radio shows and make sure we support their businesses. Money talks and if businesses thrive that support the conservative media while liberals struggle to find advertisers, you will begin seeing more and more conservative media and less and less liberal slant.

We also need to demand that the Federal Communications Commission review its standards of decency and their enforcement, and report to the president, the Congress and the American public on recent trends and prospects for the future. Concurrently, our Congress should hold hearings with representatives from the movie industry, TV producers, and the press, and begin putting pressure on them to greatly reduce the level of obscenity, sex, and violence that the media has made accessible to our children. One thing is certain: if you fill the minds of children consistently with sex and violence, your society will have massive problems with violence and promiscuous sexual activity leading to fatherless children, millions of abortions, and other innumerable and immeasurable societal problems—as ours does. America did not have anything close to today's societal problems when children were watching *The Andy Griffith Show* and were not exposed to violent and sexually explicit

TV shows, video games, and movies. This is no coincidence. Clearly, without rapid changes in our media, and in view of what the public appears willing to tolerate (and even possibly desire), we are fast becoming a modern-day Sodom and Gomorrah.

This brings us back to the values of the Founding Fathers and their vision for this country; and to the future of conservatism in America. I believe that, deep down, the vast majority of citizens feel as I do about the moral degeneration of the nation. I am certain most of our citizens want a free press focused on giving us unbiased information regarding important news events. I also believe that the large majority of Americans welcome living in a society based on sound moral principles and that is sensitive to what our children are hearing and seeing from our media. This should give us great hope and encouragement that we have the ability to change our media if we will only expend the necessary effort and determination to bring about such critical change.

★ *Part IV* ★

CONSERVATIVE SOLUTIONS TO OTHER NATIONAL CHALLENGES

A HEALTHY AMERICA

*Leave all the afternoon for exercise and recreation, which are as neces-
sary as reading¹ ...Liberty is to the collective body, what health is
to the individual body. Without health, no pleasure can be tasted
by man; without liberty, no happiness can be enjoyed by society.*²

—THOMAS JEFFERSON

J EFFERSON'S WORDS ABOUT a healthy America were echoed
almost two hundred years later by President John F. Kennedy,
who observed that physical fitness is not only one of the most
important keys to a healthy body, it is the basis of dynamic and
creative intellectual activity. In fact, Americans are extremely health-
conscious. Television advertising seems dominated by sales pitches
for all manner of drugs and cure-alls. We spend vast sums of our
tax dollars on health services, medical insurance, and advanced
research and technology. Our level of investment in health care
amounts to $2.3 trillion annually, as recently as 2008,[3] and is more
than any other industrial nation. The great irony is that, despite
this health-consciousness, the health of the average American is
poorer than that experienced by citizens of most other rich, first-
world nations. In particular, the rapid increase of obesity in our
children is a national disgrace.

Health care costs have risen dramatically over the last few decades.
They now exceed 16 percent of the nation's total gross domestic
product (GDP), and constitute an increasingly greater portion of
our federal budget.[4] Current costs are more than three times what
they were twenty years ago and nearly nine times greater than in
1980.[5] For employers, their expenditures for health care rose almost
10 percent in 2008 and they are facing a comparable rise this year.[6]

For the worker, since 1999, the average total premium for employer-sponsored health insurance has more than doubled, rising from $5,791 for family coverage to $12,680, according to a survey by the Kaiser Family Foundation and the Health Research and Educational Trust.[7] The skyrocketing costs are also sending many jobs to other countries, where costs are much lower, with India being an attractive choice for many businesses.

In 2008, 15.4 percent of Americans—approximately 46.3 million citizens—did not have medical insurance.[8] Of those who did have health insurance coverage, 29 percent were on a government insurance plan, such as Medicaid and Medicare, while 66 percent have private insurance,[9] with that number dropping rapidly due to higher unemployment and higher premiums. Employers are also moving to health insurance plans with higher deductibles to avoid high premiums, and many small businesses cannot afford to cover their employees any longer. In 2008, an estimated four million people lost their employer-sponsored health insurance.[10] By 2017, health care costs are expected to almost double to $4.3 trillion, according to the Centers for Medicare and Medicaid Services.[11] The truth is that the federal government is supposed to be defending the nation and performing the few functions states and individuals cannot perform for themselves. Instead, the federal government is fast becoming one giant, incompetent health insurance company with a few small side businesses. A recent CBO forecast showed that Medicare and Medicaid are going to take up ever-larger chunks of the federal budget, possibly reaching as high as 19 percent by 2082.[12]

PRESSING MEDICAL CHALLENGES

Our nation's most daunting health challenge is obesity. America is now home to the most obese people in the world. The U.S. Centers for Disease Control and Prevention report that obesity in adults has increased by 60 percent within the past two decades and obesity in children has tripled over the last thirty years.[13] Nearly one in three American adults is now obese,[14] and obesity-related deaths have climbed to more than three hundred thousand a year, second only to tobacco-related deaths.[15]

More than 10 percent of our health care costs are related to obesity and physical inactivity, which together trigger associated health problems, including heart disease, hypertension, diabetes, and some forms of cancer.[16] *We spend more than $175 billion a year alone on diabetes, costing us more than the wars in Iraq and Afghanistan combined!*[17] Obese and inactive workers also suffer from lower productivity, increased absenteeism, and generate high workers' compensation claims, all of which combine to lower everyone's standard of living.

This tragedy is due, in large part, to the removal of mandatory physical education and improper eating habits by our nation's children in the public school system. One of the cruelest, dumbest strategies our federal and state officials have adopted over the last thirty years has been to feed our children fattening, sugary, unhealthy foods and drinks at school and not require them or even allow them, in some cases, to exercise. In Orange County, Florida, we offer our elementary students chicken nuggets, nachos supreme, and double-stuffed-crust pizza at lunch. According to the Robert Wood Johnson Foundation, just 3.8 percent of elementary schools and 2.1 percent of high schools nationwide had daily gym class in 2006.[18] The public silence and acceptance of this very preventable tragedy is astonishing!

We seem determined to produce unhealthy young adults, many of whom have to live with horrible chronic diseases. It has been estimated that fewer than one-third of American teens spend an hour each day engaged in moderate-to-vigorous exercise. Accordingly, we need to mandate our K-12 schools to provide our children at least one hour of true aerobic activity every day. This can be accomplished by requiring all states receiving federal Medicaid payments to implement this exercise requirement. Children will welcome getting to play sports and exercise every day, and they will be much more inclined to develop an active lifestyle that will keep them healthy throughout their lives.

Our schools must also start feeding our students healthy meals. That means removing all soda and snack machines from the schools and serving nutritious lunches. Let the kids eat junk on their own time if their parents permit it, but let's not encourage bad habits by making such food items available in the schools.

Finally, nutrition should be taught for a few weeks every other school year in both our middle and high schools. Together, these steps will help head off many cases of diabetes, heart disease, hypertension, and other chronic diseases that children will otherwise suffer in later years. In the process, America's health care costs will be greatly reduced!

A second major increasing challenge is found in the rapidly growing number of Alzheimer's patients. We currently have 5.3 million Americans afflicted with Alzheimer's disease.[19] A recent report indicates that at least 11 million baby boomers, the oldest of whom will turn 65 in 2011, will develop Alzheimer's or some form of dementia.[20]

Alzheimer's and disorders like autism are becoming all too common and they will require significant resources for treatment and cures. One of the messages from this, and the health care crisis overall, is that it is incumbent on all of us to live a healthy lifestyle so that the nation maximizes its resources in the constant fight to find cures and effective treatments to fight these diseases as well as others like cancer and heart disease.

HEALTH CARE COSTS

Before discussing solutions to the crisis, we need to look at some foundational truths regarding health care that very few want to discuss. First, there exist only two choices when it comes to who will pay for your health care: either you pay your own costs, or your fellow citizens must pay for you. The government does not make money and there is no Santa Claus or magical third entity that will insure your health for free, contrary to Hillary Clinton's 2008 presidential Christmas TV ad. When the federal government pays, it is simply taking other hard-working Americans' money and giving it to you, and there is nothing American or freedom-loving about it.

Secondly, health care is a very expensive product and service. It is extremely costly for doctors to go through medical school, pharmaceutical companies to develop new products, hospitals to provide high-quality care, and companies to produce the incredible medical technologies that we take for granted today. As a result, it is critical for all of us to have access to a successful private market for health insurance whereby insurance companies can compete and spread the costs among all of us, since we usually do not know which one of us is going to need medical services. Obviously, these companies will exist only if they can make a profit.

Interestingly, liberals always complain about the outrageous profits of the "greedy" insurance and pharmaceutical companies. When I hear that complaint, my thought is always, "Why don't you liberals form your own insurance and pharmaceutical companies, charge a reasonable profit and, thus, accomplish your goal of providing cheaper health care for the nation? What's stopping you?" Moreover, if Americans continue to be increasingly afflicted with expensive chronic diseases while embracing unhealthy lifestyles, the insurance rates are going to be sky-high. Conversely, if Americans are rarely getting sick and not developing costly chronic illnesses, insurance companies will lower their premiums, since they will not have to pay out near as much in claims. The result? *Voilà!*—millions more Americans will have access to affordable health care.

This is no different than your car insurance. If we are getting in accidents all the time, either our premiums will go through the roof or insurance companies will refuse us coverage. We all know that and accept that fact. This is the essence of a free society with private markets and personal responsibility. Yet all of us seem to lose our freedom-loving, personal-responsibility instincts when it comes to health care. I wonder why? It is easy to talk about small government when it does not affect you, but when your own pocketbook is being hit, that is when you know what you truly believe and whether you really embrace the Founders' values.

For those of us who are not in favor of socialized medicine and want a free-market system to work its wonders, we need to keep these fundamental truths about our system in mind. Currently, we have a semi-private system where consumers could care less about the cost of the product (since they only pay co-pays and insurance premiums) and an unhealthy population of individuals expecting high-quality medical services at affordable rates. This is clearly not working at the moment, nor could this type of system ever work. What we have in place must be radically overhauled.

DEFICIENCIES IN THE CURRENT SYSTEM

From 2001 to 2006, the Republican-led Congress offered no health care plan. Moreover, it was as if they could not recognize a crisis when it was sitting right in front of them; or, less charitably, they really did not care, since their families and their colleagues on Capitol Hill had given themselves low-cost, high-quality health care for life. One lesson Republicans should have learned from politics in 2008 is that if the political party in charge fails to address a major crisis in America, like health care, they should not be surprised if they lose power.

John McCain did throw out one proposal: a health insurance tax credit. Very few people believed that a health insurance tax credit was going to help them significantly. Almost one-half of all Americans are not paying federal income taxes anyway and they include most of those without health insurance. Second, the insurance is so expensive and the costs are rising so fast, that no one cares about some paltry tax break. On the Democrats' side, President

Obama, Senator Reid, and Representative Pelosi seem content with an unhealthy nation, so long as we are all completely dependent on the government for health care and other social support.

Under President Obama's recent plan to nationalize health care—which we have no money to pay for and is projected to cost at least a trillion or two over the next decade—people would have little economic incentive to take care of themselves, nor would they be motivated to be efficient in their use of health care services. It is obvious that somebody else—the unknown taxpayer of future generations—will be picking up the tab.

While President Obama claims that families will still be able to stay on their current private insurance plans, clearly many Americans will leave their private plans because employers will stop paying for private health care for their employees when the employees can get care for little cost from the government. How many Americans do you think are going to stay on private health care plans and also pay for everyone else's government insurance through higher taxes? Not many that I know.

The Democrats' move toward socialized medicine also invites the inevitable, sharp decline in the amount and quality of doctors. If the Democrats are successful, there will be very few smart students going to medical school to graduate with a massive debt for the meager compensation to be offered under government-mandated reimbursement rates for their services. We already have a shortage of general surgeons as a result of a trend that is nearly thirty years long in which there are fewer and fewer surgeons per patient. We can also look forward to long lines and waiting periods for treatment, rationed care, and a drastic decline in medical advances as the private sector is inexorably eliminated from medicine. In other words, get ready for health care delivered with all the care and compassion you usually experience at your local DMV.

Moving Forward

This nation desperately needs a swift move to preventive, incentive-based, and efficient state-run private health care systems. Individuals should have significant economic incentives to live healthy lifestyles and be cost conscious when purchasing services, and our school system should aid this lifestyle effort.

With an aging population, our health care policies need to be refocused. First, we need to shift our thinking from acute care to wellness, early detection, and prevention. Of the $2 trillion spent on health care each year, less than 4 percent is spent on prevention and public health. That is completely backward. Routine childhood vaccinations result in $50 billion saved annually in direct and indirect costs. Reducing adult smoking rates by 1 percent would result in thirty thousand fewer heart attacks, sixteen thousand fewer strokes, and a savings of more than $1.5 billion over five years.[21]

Further, our citizens need to be better educated about health care options and provided with incentives, which achieve improved cost-consciousness when purchasing health care products and services. The government presently is "managing" an employer-based system within which consumers have little incentive to be cost-conscious. President Obama's plan would only further reinforce this waste and inefficiency.

Private markets can only work when consumers are price conscious. Under our current health care system or under President Obama's proposed universal coverage plan, someone else other than the consumer pays the health care bills: the government, meaning taxpayers; insurance companies; or the consumer's employer, so that costs are necessarily kept artificially high. Proof of this can be observed in the cosmetic procedures market. Such surgeries and procedures generally are not covered under health insurance plans and, thus, consumers shop for the best prices and services. Even though the demand for this service has increased more than 400 percent in the last thirteen years,[22] the real price has gone down while most other kinds of surgery have risen.

We should also emphasize and incentivize preventive medicine by giving families and individuals discounts on insurance premiums for maintaining certain weight, cholesterol, and blood pressure standards. Health care reform should address the need to prepare and incentivize our aging baby boomers to stay economically and physically active, gainfully employed, and living independently (if they so desire).

One problem we can deal with relatively quickly is reducing administrative costs. We need to shift to a computer-based paperless system for record keeping, medical billing, and prescription services, which will increase efficiency and accuracy. Most importantly, studies indicate that electronic storage and transmission of medical records will improve the care afforded patients. Systems can also be put in place to protect the privacy of these records.

In sum, smart government policy will provide incentives and tools for Americans to take responsibility for their own health while providing a world-class, efficient health care system for those in need. If we turn health care back into an area of personal, individual responsibility, the net result will be better health for all Americans and lower costs for individuals and businesses.

ENTITLEMENT REFORM

The budget should be balanced, the Treasury should be refilled,
public debt should be reduced, the arrogance of officialdom should
be tempered and controlled, and the assistance to foreign lands
should be curtailed lest Rome become bankrupt. People must
again learn to work, instead of living on public assistance.
—MARCUS T. CICERO, 55 B.C.[1]

SOCIAL SECURITY REFORM

WHEN HISTORIANS LOOK back at 2008, they will recall that it was the year in which Bernie Madoff became a household name and the American public redis-covered the Ponzi scheme. Both Charles Ponzi in the 1920s and Madoff today followed the same approach: convince the public to invest their money with the promise of a guaranteed astonishingly high rate of return. These early investors would, in turn, be paid with funds contributed by later investors. It all worked well for a while. The pyramid grew taller until the number of new investors attracted to the scheme became too few to cover the payments to those who preceded them.

It is ironic, to the point of being amusing, that the many Ameri-cans who are shaking their heads today about how so many of their fellow citizens could be so gullible as to be taken in by Madoff are themselves participants in the world's largest and longest-running Ponzi scheme—welcome to the U.S. Social Security program. In 2008 alone, working Americans paid more than $800 billion into Social Security and its various programs.[2]

The principal difference is that Congress is the fund manager for

Social Security, not Madoff or Ponzi. And Congress certainly has it much better. Unlike voluntary investment schemes, with Social Security, all investors are required to contribute under the law. Second, when the system collapses under its weight in the future, our congressional managers of today will likely be gone from the scene and far from the arm of the law or the wrath of the public. But, just like Madoff and Ponzi, our elected officials can dip into the fund of investor contributions and spend it willy-nilly, without investors knowing what is happening. And, they do it with relish.

In 1983, President Reagan and the Democrat Congress raised Social Security taxes to create short-term surpluses designed to deal eventually with millions of baby boomers who would begin retiring in 2010 and beyond. Sadly, our Congress has been raiding billions and billions of those surpluses since then to pay for their own pet projects. Today, there is no pile of money invested or saved to pay these benefits as promised. Because of congressional mismanagement and outright stealing of those funds, our Social Security system is rapidly going broke.

Social Security was intended to provide a "safety net" for poor, elderly citizens to prevent them from becoming impoverished. The U.S. Social Security program is, today, the largest such program in the world, and the single largest expenditure in the federal budget, surpassing Medicare/Medicaid and military expenditures.[3] One primary reason for this is that people are living longer on average than when the system was created seventy-five years ago, placing ever-greater strain on the system.

Congress established a trust fund in the U.S. Treasury to account for all program income and disbursements to Social Security and survivor beneficiaries. In 2008, the Social Security Trust Fund received $805 billion in income.[4] Beyond the $672 billion in payroll taxes (contributed on a 50:50 basis by employees and employers), the fund received $116 billion in interest on past contributions and $17 billion from the taxes beneficiaries pay on their Social Security income.[5]

Don't think, however, that your contributions are ending up in any type of lockbox in the U.S. Treasury for safekeeping until you retire. Any surplus that remains after the current retirees are paid is kept in U.S. government bonds. The money ends up in the Treasury's general revenue fund for the government's deficit spending. In effect, the Trust Fund is stuffed with IOUs that we all better hope the government can make good on when it is our turn to step up to the payment window.

Social Security faces a serious deficit over the long term because the ratio of payroll-tax-paying workers to benefit-collecting retirees is declining, especially with the coming retirement of the baby-boomer generation. When Social Security was first established, the payroll taxes of forty-one workers supported one retiree who, on average, did not have a long life span. We are now down to three workers for each retiree and soon the ratio will reach 2.2 workers to 1 retiree.[6] In 2000, we had thirty-five million Americans aged sixty-five and over, and in 2040 this number will skyrocket to 70 million.[7]

According to the government's own analysis, by 2016 we will have reached the point where outlays from the Social Security Trust Fund begin to exceed the amount of annual tax revenue.[8] We are quite likely to be running larger deficits much sooner than envisioned earlier. Projections indicate that by 2037, the Trust Fund will be exhausted.[9]

Our current and future Social Security beneficiaries face two risks: one is that our spendthrift Congress will not be able to make good on the IOUs (in Treasury bonds) held in the Trust Fund. The other and more likely downside is that sometime in the next thirty years there will be inadequate funds available for the government to pay Social Security benefits as promised.

SOLUTIONS

According to the latest report by the Fund trustees, Social Security could be brought into balance over the next seventy-five years in various ways, including an immediate increase of 16 percent in payroll taxes (from the current 12.4 percent of wages to 14.4 percent), an immediate reduction in benefits of 13 percent, or some combination thereof.[10] Further, ensuring the solvency of the system beyond the next seventy-five years would require even larger changes due to an aging population and increasing longevity. Any of these options are totally unacceptable, in my view. Retirees are already struggling to make ends meet and individuals and businesses are already overtaxed.

In 2005, President George Bush proposed a series of changes to solve the crisis. They included a transformation of Social Security based on allowing younger workers to invest some of their payroll taxes in regulated individual retirement accounts. This would, in effect, give them ownership of personal accounts (mutual funds but not individual stocks) with higher rates of return and better future retirement benefits than are possible under the current system.

Bush understood, as did anyone else paying attention to the current situation, that it did not make sense to force young workers into reliance on a system that is not sustainable, given the country's demographics and the Congress' penchant to spend every dime as soon as it arrives in Washington, if not sooner. If you cared about personal freedom, individual rights, and about the future of our workers and their children, you loved Bush's plan.

The plan would not have affected the millions of Americans who rely on the current program and it did not force anybody to make any changes. What it would do is help young workers opt out of the existing system that will definitely fail them unless changed. Yet Congress took no action, maybe because it would give government less control of peoples' lives and their money. Moreover, people might actually be able to create wealth on their own and not need the government, God forbid! More depressingly, the public did not rally behind the plan. We sure look like we love freedom every Fourth of July, waving our flags, but in reality I am not so sure the Founders would be impressed by our love for freedom and personal responsibility if we do not even trust ourselves enough to save and/ or invest our own money. How this could happen in a country that supposedly reveres freedom, personal choice, and individual rights? I do not know, but it happened. Thus, Congress will continue to tax individuals and businesses at least 12.4 percent of their wages each paycheck, while they spend any surpluses the next few years on any programs they want. Yet liberals and the media constantly argue what a great risk it is to have workers put their money into mutual funds or other investments. Oh, yes, their Ponzi scheme clearly is risk free.

I suggest we consider a similar alternative to President Bush's plan, where workers, at their option, invest much of their money in regulated, diverse investment accounts (part stocks, bonds, or CDs). Here, the government would guarantee your Social Security principal contributions, which would be insured by the government in case of any market downturn and losses. This would allay much of the fear that potential stock market losses would wipe out one's retirement.

At least your money, instead of being stolen by Congress for earmarks, could be invested in the private market so that our Social Security system would not go bankrupt and most people could make a reasonable return on their money. Currently, inflation in food, gas, and health care costs are making retirees' Social Security checks look quite meager. Through privatization of the system, we would infuse a tremendous amount of money into our economy and stock market, greatly increasing the value of all of our 401(k) plans and other investments.

If we will not move toward private accounts, we must raise the age of eligibility for retirement benefits very gradually over the next twenty years, since we are living fourteen years longer than when the system was introduced in the 1930s.

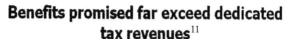

Benefits promised far exceed dedicated tax revenues[11]

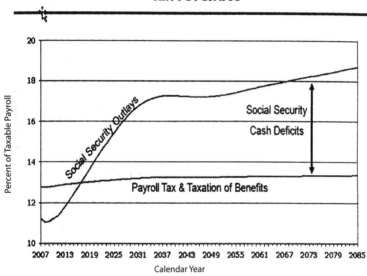

MEDICARE

If you came away feeling depressed after reading about Social Security, you probably should skip this section. The problems with Medicare are both more severe and more immediate. In 2008, for the first time, Medicare's Hospital Insurance (HI) Trust Fund paid out more in hospital benefits and associated expenditures than it received in payroll taxes and interest.[12] Medicare was created in 1965 as part of Lyndon Johnson's Great Society program. The first beneficiary card was given to an earlier President, Harry S. Truman. The Social Security administration originally administered Medicare, but in 1973 its management was shifted to the Health Care Financing administration of the Department of Health and Human

Services (and now called the Centers for Medicare and Medicaid Services). The original Medicare plan had Parts A and B components, the former covering hospital treatment and the latter physician service. In January 2006, a Part D was added to cover prescription drugs. Coverage is provided to U.S. citizens sixty-five years and older, to younger people receiving Social Security benefits, and to persons requiring kidney dialysis or transplants. According to the Social Security Trustees report, in 2008, approximately 166 million people paid taxes from their incomes into Medicare.[13] Total Medicare spending (Parts A, B, and D) amounted to a staggering $468 billion in 2008, and the costs are projected to climb rapidly.[14]

As with Social Security, the revenues generated to cover claims come principally from three sources: payroll taxes shared between employees and employers, interest paid on accumulated revenue, and taxes paid by beneficiaries on benefits received. In the case of Medicare, the revenue is held in two trust funds: one for Part A, and a second for Parts B and D. And as with Social Security, both of the funds are in trouble. In the case of Part A, 2008 marked the first year that payouts exceeded revenues. As early as 2017, the trust fund will be completely depleted.[15] And, as with Social Security, there is no provision to enable full payment of benefits after the fund has been exhausted. Unless the system is reformed, the level of payment to beneficiaries will depend solely on the volume of payroll taxes collected each year.

In the case of the trust fund for Medicare Parts B and D, the situation is somewhat different, since the major source of income is the government's general revenue, a source unavailable to either the Social Security Fund or the Medicare Hospital Insurance Fund. The problem here is that the rapidly rising costs of Parts B and D are placing growing strains on the federal general revenue that funds the rest of the government's operations.

The bottom line is that Medicare's financial difficulties come sooner and are much more severe than those confronting Social Security. While both programs face demographic challenges related to the aging of our population, with fewer workers covering more retirees, Medicare has a special problem of being severely impacted by rapidly rising health care costs. In the case of Social Security, beyond 2030 the gap between payroll tax revenues and beneficiary payouts will widen only slightly. With Medicare, while tax revenues remain fairly constant, program costs are projected to rise dramatically.

What can be done to rectify this situation? Just as with Social Security, there is no painless magic bullet to employ. It again will require our political leaders in Washington to show leadership and courage. There are few choices, beyond just muddling on, continuing to kick the can down the road, and hoping that the crisis hits full-bore on someone else's watch. These are the options: more revenue must be generated through (choke!) higher payroll taxes; or, we must extend the age at which workers become eligible for benefits; and/or, benefits will have to be reduced.

I am strongly against raising taxes or decreasing benefits for retirees and, therefore, favor gradually increasing the elegibility age for workers under fifty-five to preserve the system. To save Medicare, we must also be able to sustain strong economic growth or we will simply run out of money, which is another reason we must switch to the Fair Tax to protect our seniors' benefits.

It is painfully obvious that the federal government is not capable of running giant government programs such as Medicare either effectively or efficiently. There is no accountability built into the programs and the waste of taxpayer dollars is a national scandal. Medicare fraud costs Americans more than $60 billion a year![16] That is why I believe all health care programs, including Medicare and Medicaid, should be funded by each state with local control and oversight. The truth is that local officials are more accountable. Our health care system would be much better and more efficiently run if the states managed their own Medicare-styled programs.

The only reason for the federal government to be involved in health care is so one generation can rob from the next, not because the federal government runs an efficient, effective program. Of course, many Americans, and certainly the politicians, embrace the thought of a benevolent federal government taking care of the citizen's every need, no matter what the cost and who bears it.

I also believe that if certain liberal states like California want to have a single payer system with coverage for all, they should do so. If other states' residents want free market care, they should have that system without federal government interference. There is no reason we have to have a one-system-fits-all mentality, centrally commanded and controlled by Washington. Why don't we let each state decide how they want to run their health care system? Once again, I know whose side Washington, Jefferson, Franklin, and Adams would be on in this debate.

One final point: Liberals would hate this idea because they know most of the good doctors would practice in the free market states and that all of the wealth creators and job producers would flee their socialist health care system states leaving the remaining states with no money to fund their beloved programs.

MEDICARE FRAUD

Our Congress is responsible for ensuring that our taxpayer dollars are treated with respect and spent wisely. Sadly, tens of billions are lost every year to fraud from poorly managed government programs. Law enforcement estimates put the widespread schemes that bilk Medicare at an estimated $60 billion a year,[17] a staggering cost borne by American taxpayers.

The scale of Medicare fraud and abuse is immense. The Inspector General of the U.S. Department of Health and Human Services revealed that 72 percent of the Medicare claims submitted nationwide for HIV/AIDS treatment in 2005 came from South Florida.[18] What is especially revealing and shocking about this revelation is that only 8 percent of the country's HIV/AIDS Medicare beneficiaries actually live in South Florida.[19] In the words of one federal official, the level of fraud was "off the charts." In response, the U.S. Justice Department last year set up a strike force at a remote office near Miami. In just six months, prosecutors filed 74 cases, charging 120 people with stealing $400 million from Medicare.[20]

One common scheme is illicit billings, for example, for durable medical equipment such as oxygen generators, breathing machines, air mattresses, walkers, orthopedic braces, and wheel chairs. This alone has been estimated to be costing American taxpayers billions of dollars a year in illegal claims. In another example, federal officials described a case involving an electric wheelchair that cost five thousand dollars. By repeatedly billing Medicare, criminals defrauded the system for $5 million without ever delivering the item.[21]

If the federal government is going to be so heavily involved in health care, it has a responsibility to make sure that the system is run efficiently. Currently, Medicare spends only, "two-tenths of a cent of every dollar in its $456 billion annual budget on waste, abuse and fraud problems,"[22] and there are few incentives for responsible government employees to do a good job in identifying and combating Medicare fraud and abuse. By contrast, HMOs spend significantly more, and their employees have financial incentives to do their jobs well. A healthy investment in an effective fraud department with financial incentives for its staff seems like a no-brainer to me at a time when Congress' current alternative permits $60 billion to be siphoned off by criminals each year. The old maxim, "You get what you pay for," is certainly true here.

Repowering the United States:
The Energy Challenge

*A country can only be free if it can do three
things...feed itself, ...fuel itself...fight for itself.*
—Governor Mike Huckabee[1]

F OR THE LAST several decades, our nation has been facing
a growing energy crisis. As of 2009, America continues
to import 53 percent of its oil and petroleum products as
hundreds of billions of dollars leave our economy each year;[2] and
everyone seems ready for serious action on the energy front, except
our politicians in Washington. We should not be too surprised that
we have high unemployment rates and no money to pay our bills if
we let five hundred billion dollars a year leave the country year after
year because we have no effective energy policy.

This is not a crisis of nature. There is plenty of energy in the
U.S. that is just not being used. It is a crisis of political will and
commitment. For decades, our politicians have made loud noises
about how they would lead us to energy independence. In actuality,
they have done virtually nothing as they remain beholden to special
interest groups, as the contributions to their political campaigns
and other favors roll in.

I particularly fault members of my own party, who, from 2001 to
2006, had an excellent opportunity to begin launching new nuclear
power plants, increasing our drilling for oil and natural gas on and
offshore, and putting together a coherent national energy plan as
the energy crisis worsened considerably. Republicans, instead, blew
their opportunity and took little constructive action. They also

failed miserably in standing up to the industry lobbyists and energy subsidy seekers and especially in defending free-market principles as the best and most efficient means for ensuring that this nation has a secure supply of energy at affordable prices.

We continue to ignore, at our peril, just how dependent this nation is on energy availability. It drives the engine of our economic growth and lies at the heart of the high standard of living Americans have enjoyed. Available energy at low cost is something that Americans had taken for granted for decades until the oil shocks of the seventies and nineties put that to rest. We really woke up when the price of oil reached an all-time high of $147 a barrel in 2008 and gasoline cost upward of $4 a gallon that summer.[3]

Despite these facts, we now have elected a president who does not want to increase drilling for oil or natural gas and detests coal usage due to his global warming concerns. Moreover, he shows no interest in building new nuclear facilities due to waste storage concerns. He tells us that we can become 50 percent more energy independent in ten years without doing any of these things, but simply investing in alternative energy sources and increasing our fuel efficiency. Let's look at the facts.

OIL DEPENDENCY

Our energy crisis stems from our heavy dependence on fossil fuels, which constitute 84 percent of our total energy usage (oil, 37 percent; natural gas, 24 percent; and coal, 23 percent)[4] Other than fossil fuels, nuclear energy provides 9 percent of the energy mix, with the remaining 7 percent coming from a variety of renewable sources: predominantly hydroelectric and biomass, with wind energy, solar power, and geothermal providing modest contributions.[5] Remember this fact because President Obama apparently believes he can turn this 7 percent number into at least 50 percent in ten years. I doubt it can even become 20 percent, and we will still be importing as much oil as ever.

Our daily demand of oil in 2008 was almost 19 million barrels each day.[6] Seventy-one percent of the oil used today in the U.S. is to power our cars, trucks, and busses.[7] The crucial concern, of course, is that we do not produce enough oil within our own country to meet our needs, nor do other ready domestic alternatives exist. We do remain one of the major oil producers in the world, accounting for nearly 8 percent of global oil production in 2008,[8] but this is a dramatic reduction from the U.S. share of worldwide output in recent decades. And this decline is expected to continue. As a consequence, the U.S. has turned to other countries to fill the gap. Today we import more than half of the oil our economy requires at a total cost of nearly a half trillion dollars each year, depending on how much the price of a barrel of oil fluctuates.[9] Every dollar is the taxpayer's money that could certainly find better uses. Ever forecast indicates these numbers will continue to increase.

Even more serious, we have managed through past inaction to place ourselves at the mercy of other governments, many of which are unstable or unfriendly. Fortunately, our two immediate neighbors provide one-third of our petroleum imports: Canada, 12.8 percent; and Mexico, 7 percent.[10] Beyond this, the picture is not a pretty one. The next three leading crude-oil exporters to the U.S. are Saudi Arabia, Venezuela, and Nigeria.[11] We also rely on Russia for refined crude oil and other petroleum products on a daily basis.

If there is any good news on the oil front, it is that there are good possibilities for significantly increasing U.S. domestic production. The lower forty-eight states have recoverable oil on federally owned lands estimated in the billions barrels, according to the U.S. Geological Survey and the Minerals Management Service. This would mean a healthy additional proportion to the total oil reserves estimated to exist in the U.S. overall. However, access to these reserves is restricted because of their location which has, to date, placed them off limits to exploration and development, or at least subject to considerable exploration and development restrictions.

Drilling restrictions onshore include a portion of the Arctic

National Wildlife Refuge (ANWR) in Alaska, known as the "1002 Area." If the American Energy Independence and Price Reduction Act, proposed in Spring 2008, was passed, a very small section of ANWR's 19 million acres would be opened for drilling. This 1002 Area is estimated to hold approximately 7 billion barrels of recoverable oil.[12]

With respect to drilling and exploitation offshore of the U.S., this is currently prohibited in all areas along the North Atlantic coast, most of the Pacific Coast, part of the Alaskan coast, and most of the eastern Gulf of Mexico, despite the fact that there is at least 19 billion barrels of recoverable oil lying untouched in the restricted areas.[13] Drilling is permitted only in the Western Gulf of Mexico and some parts of Alaska. Nonetheless, in 2008, offshore production still constituted 6 percent of total domestic production, a percentage that has been climbing as oil production onshore has decreased.[14]

As the search for more domestic production has intensified in recent years, producers have moved to ever-deeper offshore locations and have explored unconventional sources such as oil shale (abundant in the western U.S.) and oil sands. Development of these unconventional sources, however, comes with increased production costs and the requirement to overcome considerable technological and environmental hurdles. The extraction of oil from oil shale, for example, consumes very large quantities of energy and water.

Finally, we must begin building new oil refineries, as well as enlarge existing plants. Democrats have consistently resisted all such efforts. For thirty years we have failed to build new refineries and are now paying a heavy price.

NATURAL GAS

Natural gas, a clean burning fuel used largely for electrical generators and residential heating, currently accounts for close to 25 percent of the total U.S. energy supply.[15] Our nation is one of the largest gas producers in the world, with more than 88 percent of our demand supplied by domestic production.[16]

Our natural gas opportunities are, however, tremendously under-utilized. For example, Alaska could provide part of U.S. gas demand if the state's existing resources were fully developed. Recently, there have been many large natural gas fields discovered in Pennsylvania and other states. Studies of modern drilling techniques to recover natural gas from shale deposits under Texas, Louisiana, Arkansas, and Appalachia indicate we may have more than a one hundred-year supply of natural gas, with at least that much more off our coasts. T. Boone Pickens, the Texas oil billionaire who has become famous for his national television ads promoting increased investments in alternative energy sources, cites our underutilization of our natural gas supplies as one of America's greatest energy failures.

Congressional opposition and red tape has combined to deter full exploration of our natural gas resources. Another constraint is local concern about the environmental impacts of exploratory and production drilling. Many Democrats, including President Obama, seem opposed to any energy source that emits carbon dioxide into the air, supposedly due to global-warming concerns. The tragic part of our failure to develop this great natural resource is that natural gas is, by far, the cleanest-burning fossil fuel. As such, as a replacement for oil and coal, natural gas reduces greenhouse gas emissions while giving us a bona fide existing source of abundant, affordable, reliable energy.

For whatever reason, the Democrats would rather have America import dirtier fossil fuels, like oil, from hostile nations and send taxpayer dollars overseas than use much cleaner natural gas and keep taxpayer dollars in taxpayer hands, while creating more jobs here in America. One can only ask why the Democrats favor such a destructive course.

CLEANER COAL

Coal is our most abundant fuel. The U.S. has the largest coal reserves in the world, possessing resources accounting for more than 28 percent of the worldwide total.[17] Coal is also very cheap compared to oil and gas alternatives. The U.S., not surprisingly, is a net exporter of coal. Exports nearly doubled between 1973 and 1990, reaching 100 million tons in 1991 before falling back to 1973 levels by 2006 when exports stood at 45 million tons.[18] At the same time, U.S. imports of coal have increased as our demand for cheaper coal from foreign sources grows, along with the desire for low-sulfur, cleaner coal found outside the U.S.

Developments in climate change policy and the possibility of a cost being attached to CO^2 emissions through a carbon tax or cap-and-trade system are, undoubtedly, slowing construction in new coal-fired power plants, this despite impressive investment plans by utilities. Eliminating or reducing these uncertainties will be necessary to ensure that coal can continue to play a key role in providing fuel diversity and security in the U.S.

The problem is that coal is the dirtiest of our fuels, in terms of the air pollutants emitted during its combustion, and its mining often leaves behind extensive despoiled landscapes. Due to advanced technologies for emission control and for mining, this situation is improving and any future U.S. national energy plan must promote further advancement of clean coal technology.

As it is, the U.S. Department of Energy has stated that recent advances will cut sulfur, nitrogen, and mercury pollutants from coal-fired power plants by nearly 70 percent by the year 2018.[19] There are already four plants in operation nationally that use advanced clean coal technology, including one in Tampa, Florida, that appear economically viable. California has plans to develop huge new coal-fired electrical generating plants that are low-polluting.

Finally, while we have the technology to trap much of the carbon dioxide emitted from coal plants, building these facilities and implementing these technologies across the numerous coal-fired power plants in our nation would include massive additional cost, in excess of trillions. This is the primary reason why carbon-trapping technologies are not being utilized. Accordingly, the global warming believers, including President Obama, are unlikely to see coal as a useful energy source moving forward, unless the government decides to print more money for this cause as well.

RENEWABLE ENERGY

The pathway toward energy independence for the U.S. should involve carving out a larger role for renewable sources. The problem, however, is that as recently as 2008 renewable sources constitute only 7 percent of the nation's total energy supply and 9 percent of electricity production.[20] The U.S. Department of Energy expects this rate to continue expanding. The main components of renewable energy in this country are hydropower (34 percent of the total), biomass (53 percent), geothermal (6 percent), wind (7 percent), and solar (1 percent).[21]

Meanwhile, President Obama continues trying to lead Americans into believing that the U.S. can become energy independent simply by investing in more renewable energy and conservation. Remember the above current percentages the next time President Obama tells you how he is going to make us 50 percent more energy independent in ten years without using nuclear energy or increased domestic drilling for natural gas and oil. With our need for energy increasing every year, any serious energy independence plan must include increased domestic fossil fuel use, nuclear energy, and other sources outside of renewable energy.

The most rapidly growing renewable source in the U.S. is wind power for electricity generation. It almost doubled between 2006 and 2008, contributing almost 2 percent of the nation's total electricity.[22] This was mainly due to newly constructed wind power plants. Because of significant advances in generation technology, both in the U.S. and other nations, the cost of producing electricity from wind power in the U.S. has dropped from eighty cents per kilowatt hour in 1980 to between five and eight cents today.[23]

A major constraint on growth is the large investment needed to develop the transmission infrastructure to carry the wind-derived power from its place of origin to the nation's principal electrical grid. Further, there is strong environmental opposition by some in Congress who feel that, while one windmill is quaint, a landscape or seascape dotted with large wind propellers is anything but.

The U.S. is also increasing its use of biomass (plant matter that can be converted to fuel), principally as a substitute for petroleum in the transport sector. In his 2007 State of the Union address, President Bush announced a long-term plan to further increase the contribution of biofuels to the supply of transportation energy, with a goal of having the production of biofuels and other alternative fuels reach 35 billion gallons by 2017.[24]

Growth of biofuel production has increased faster than expected as recently as five years ago, driven by large subsidies awarded to farmers, corporations, and petroleum refiners for the production of corn-based ethanol, which is then blended with gasoline. To further support this industry, a special tariff was applied by the U.S. to prevent the import of cheaper ethanol abroad, principally from Brazil's sugar cane-derived ethanol. This corn-to-ethanol program, unfortunately, highlights some of the worst aspects of our government's heavy-handedness in the energy market, providing billions of dollars in subsidies for ethanol that made barely a dent in our energy demand. Most egregiously, however, this has caused wheat and corn farmers to convert their food-producing croplands to corn-ethanol energy-producing fields, which caused a dramatic increase in our food prices.

We need to suspend the subsidized ethanol program to put more corn and wheat back into the food supply and to encourage farmers to plant other crops. It is important to note that ethanol can and should be made from many sources other than corn or sugars, including citrus waste, woodchips, and other nonfood materials.

THE NUCLEAR OPTION

In the face of our growing energy demand and the search of greater security of supply, nuclear energy is getting another look in the U.S. and worldwide. This is seen most dramatically in countries like Denmark, Sweden, and Germany, which just a decade ago were foreswearing a nuclear-based energy future.

As surprising as it may be to many Americans, the U.S. has the world's largest number of nuclear power plants. There are at present 104 units operating across 31 states. Combined, they provide 19 percent or our total electricity production. This output is in stark contrast to the situation in France, where nuclear power constitutes 79 percent of their nation's electricity. Other countries where nuclear meets a significant proportion of overall national energy demand include Japan, 28 percent; Germany, 27 percent; and the U.K., 20 percent.[25]

It has now been more than thirty years since the U.S. began construction of a new nuclear plant, mainly due to strong opposition by environmental activists. This has begun to change as concerns have grown about our over-reliance on foreign sources of energy and also about global warming, with nuclear energy offering an alternative to greenhouse gas-producing fossil fuels. Thus, the licenses of existing U.S. plants are being extended and utilities are planning to seek authorization for new facilities. Further, the Tennessee Valley Authority has resumed construction of Unit 2 of its Watts Bar plant in eastern Tennessee, which was suspended in 1988 when 60 percent complete.

Overall, plans are in the works for between four and eight new power plants to begin operation by 2018, with as many as twenty-six new nuclear units in the U.S. in the next few decades, and seventeen licensing applications for additional new plants submitted by late 2009.[26] During the last presidential campaign, John McCain called for the construction of forty-five nuclear reactors by 2030, with a longer-term goal of adding an additional fifty-five.[27] I strongly support Senator McCain's proposal.

America has the technology to build safe and cost-effective nuclear plants, and this CO_2-free power source must be used as part of our overall strategy for energy security. Despite the exemplary safety record of the nuclear industry in the U.S. and abroad over the past three decades, public opposition continues in many quarters. Some relates to the not-in-my-backyard mentality of local citizens fearful of possible accidents. Much of the opposition concerns the matter of the waste-disposal challenge. The operating U.S. nuclear power plants produce some two thousand tons of used fuel annually. This is currently stored on-site in water-filled pools or in dry storage flasks. Many nations use nuclear reprocessing which converts the waste to almost nothing and can be stored on site and have done so very safely.

Unfortunately, until very recently, President Obama and the Democrats have shown no inclination to build any nuclear plants or increase our usage of nuclear energy. Thus, our politicians continue to allow hundreds of billions of dollars to continue to leave our economy annually (despite the tremendous loss of jobs and wealth we are already suffering from) for foreign lands despite having safe, effective nuclear technology to help prevent Americans from suffering from this downward economic spiral.

WHAT DOES THIS ALL MEAN AND WHAT IS THE BEST WAY FORWARD?

It is clear that our economic growth will continue to require an increasing amount of energy to keep it going. Further, despite significant possibilities for meeting future demand with greater contributions from nuclear energy, renewables, and other unconventional sources, their cumulative contribution to America's energy mix over the next two to three decades will remain relatively small. Thus, this nation will have to continue to rely on fossil fuels to keep the economy running.

Fortunately, there are many steps we can and should take to free us from our reliance on foreign oil and afford us greater political and economic stability. The bad news is that this will require vision, courage and intelligence from our politicians in Washington, attributes currently in very short supply.

My view of the way forward is the following:

1. We must develop a comprehensive, long-term national plan for energy security with goals, mandates, and targets. It must have at its center the goal of breaking our addiction to oil, which now places our national security at risk. Such a national plan should set out the roles of the federal government and the states and provide a mechanism for cooperation and coordination. To date, our Congress and successive administrations have provided, through periodic acts, a piecemeal idea-du-jour approach to a matter of strategic importance to the nation's future.

2. Our Congress must promote a market-based approach to energy exploration and development. It must renounce the use of subsidies (especially ethanol), which distort the marketplace, along with trade barriers that protect inefficient U.S. energy producers and reward pet lobbyists.

3. We must develop America's indigenous fossil fuels, especially natural gas, which should be the most politically popular given the fact it is the cleanest of the fossil fuels. Specifically, I support offshore drilling and the removal of the 1990 moratorium on exploratory drilling and production off Florida's coast and other currently restricted areas. It is estimated that there is enough oil

off America's coastlines to fuel millions cars for decades. If Hurricane Katrina can plow through a field of oil and gas rigs without a major disaster, then we have our evidence that drilling offshore can be done safely. Development of ANWR and our abundant oil shale reserves must also be explored.

These steps, taken together, will give our economy a tremendous boost and keep taxpayer dollars here in the U.S. Increased use of domestic fossil fuels must serve as a bridge for the next several decades as we develop battery-powered cars, new technologies and turn more and more to renewable sources of energy.

4. Nuclear energy must also be a much larger part of our future energy mix. The industry has proven that, based on new fail-safe systems, nuclear plants can be operated safely over long periods. Public acceptance requires resolving the waste-disposal problem. The U.S. should launch a modern-day *Manhattan Project* on nuclear-waste disposal to help eliminate risks and alleviate concerns, an effort possibly carried out in cooperation with other countries.

5. We must substantially intensify our efforts to reduce energy demand through programs to improve energy efficiency in our homes, in the workplace and on the highway. With a strong push to curb demand through policies which increase energy efficiency, especially in transport, we can save Americans money needlessly spent on energy as well as accomplishing our energy security and environmental goals.

The key is to bring on line a new generation of vehicles powered by electricity, hydrogen, and possibly solar radiation. Electric vehicles are now in production, and Toyota, Chevrolet, Honda, and Volkswagen all have announced plans to produce zero-emission hydrogen fuel-cell cars. Technology exists for the manufacturing of electric cars and many are ready for distribution by 2010. Chevrolet is working on development of the Chevy Volt, an electric vehicle using a lithium-ion battery. A common 110-volt household plug can charge this vehicle. For trips of fewer than forty miles, it uses zero gasoline and produces zero emissions. For longer trips, a small, range-extending gasoline engine recharges the battery.[28] Providing major tax incentives for advancements in this technology can ensure mass production of battery-powered vehicles in the near future.

Here, government can play a critical role by encouraging inventors and manufacturers who are working to develop more powerful batteries and improved fuel cells with tax credits, guarantees and other incentives. Increased use of mass transit systems is a key component of this strategy, as well.

6. Related to the supply side of our future energy strategy is the issue of the role of renewable energy sources. The government must give solar, wind, and biomass technologies and industries a fair chance in the marketplace. It should substitute subsidies for mature energy corporations with expanded research and development support for unconventional energy development. Given America's strong research and development capacity, our "Yankee ingenuity," and time-honored "Can Do" spirit, there is no reason the U.S. cannot become the world leader in the field of renewables, gaining market shares as well as enhanced energy security at the same time.

18

Environmental Ethics and Conservative Values

The rules of the game are what we call Nature. The player on the other side is hidden from us. We know that his play is always fair, just and patient. But also we know, to our cost, that he never overlooks a mistake, or makes the smallest allowance for ignorance.

—Thomas Huxley[1]

THERE ARE MANY words that come to mind as I contemplate this subject: *disappointed, frustrated,* and *stunned* that the Republican Party, again, has no discernible position on protecting our environment and where our efforts should be focused. Currently, conservatives and the Republican Party are widely perceived within the electorate as anti-environment ideologues. This is largely due to liberal media and educational institutions. But it is also the result of our own failures. On practical grounds, this is no way to attract young or undecided voters to the cause.

Be that as it may, unfortunately and needlessly, in recent years Republicans have placed themselves in the public's eye as being at odds with protection of the environment. The public rarely, if ever, sees Republicans fighting to protect the environment. What really hurts is that Republicans have had a long history of championing policies and programs designed to protect natural resources and environmental quality.

Some one hundred years ago, President Teddy Roosevelt personified America's environmental ethic by establishing the first national parks and the U.S. Forest Service. At the beginning of the seventies, President Richard Nixon's first statutory act was to sign into law the National Environmental Policy Act, which established the EPA and the Environmental Impact Statement procedure. In the 1980s, President Ronald Reagan launched an international effort to protect the earth's ozone layer from depletion due to refrigerants such as Freon and other man-made chemicals.

In subsequent years, however, the environmental high ground has been claimed by liberals in this country who proclaim that Republicans treat the earth like a cheap hotel and just want it to hold together long enough until they check out. While this is liberal nonsense, it is true that in staking out positions on economic growth and international accords, conservatives have too often placed themselves in opposition to environmental initiatives that capture strong public support. A case in point is the matter of regulatory reform. In calling for a reduction in the regulatory burden industry was facing, President Reagan spoke of improving the quality of regulation, not its complete elimination. To this day, however, Republicans are viewed as being opposed to virtually all environmental regulations, an attitude especially evident during periods of economic downturn.

An additional aspect of this is the Republicans' relationship with industry and corporate America. Republicans are seen as being completely supportive of industry, however it behaves, and any impediment that might be placed in the path toward economic growth is to be challenged and overcome. This perception exists despite the fact that, on many occasions, our industrial firms have misbehaved and been neglectful of health and environmental consequences of their actions.

Our history is replete with situations involving pesticide poisonings, birth defects from Thalidomide, Freon destruction of the ozone layer, and the toxic effects of tobacco and asbestos, in which industry has initially denied all responsibility and obtained the support of Republicans in their denials, only to later retract their positions in the face of scientific evidence. The problem is not that conservatives identify themselves with industry and continually point to the necessary truth that a strong America depends upon a strong industrial base, but that too many Republicans have given knee-jerk support for industry's behavior, regardless of egregious mistakes.

Let me suggest several steps that conservatives can take to recapture some of the high ground in environmental affairs, or at least not be perceived as uncaring and reactionary:

1. For Christian conservatives, we must recognize that God's call upon man to replenish the earth and to exercise dominion over the sea, land, and all living things (Gen. 1:28) surely means that we are entrusted with responsibility for the planet's stewardship and long-term well-being. Acknowledgement of this responsibility must undergird our perspective on environmental matters.

2. Conservatives have long argued for balanced budgets so that we do not mortgage the well-being of our children and future generations. We must also recognize and proclaim that this level of concern also extends to the quality of the environment we leave to our children. It is worth considering the old saying, "Of what value is a home if one doesn't have a decent planet on which to place it?"

3. We also have to get beyond the feeling that environmental concerns are the prerogative of the liberals and that an expression of concern about dirty air or dirty water means associating ourselves with the positions of alarmist Hollywood types and environmental extremists. Conservatives clearly share an interest with liberals in protecting air, water, and natural resources and we should speak with a strong voice and take the lead on protecting the environment when appropriate.

4. Republicans must also break out of this "all regulation is bad," "whatever industry does is right" mentality. On some occasion, industry does destroy our environment and must be regulated or stopped altogether. Moreover, such blind allegiance to industry's positions, regardless of their truthfulness, is killing the image that Republicans must project to the general public if we are to be taken seriously on environmental issues and thus regain our position and influence in public affairs. Certainly, a change in approach and language can be introduced into the discourse without sacrificing core beliefs and values.

You may ask: what about global warming or climate change? My response is, always seek truth from whatever source (and always consider the source, of course), and we will have to save that topic for a book of its own.

I will say President Obama's carbon tax policy—a.k.a. the *cap-and-trade* scheme—would be disastrous for this nation. It would further hurt consumers, particularly our seniors and the poor who would see their utility bills rise dramatically, as well as further damage the overall economy.

19

Ending Illegal Immigration

The execution of the laws is more important than the making of them.

—Thomas Jefferson[1]

THE UNITED STATES is a nation of immigrants. The *Statute of Liberty's* lamp-bearing hand raised high above Ellis Island is one of our nation's enduring symbols. People from all walks of life and from all corners of the world—the tired, poor, and huddled masses that yearn to breathe free—who have immigrated here over the past 230 years have made America the industrious, creative, and vibrant nation that is the envy of the world. We must continue to welcome individuals from other lands, giving priority to those who can and are willing to advance the nation's interests and common good. Immigrants and temporary workers who play by the rules deserve to be treated fairly and with dignity.

The problem we face, however, is that there are many reaching our country today, and in growing numbers, who are not playing by the rules. Most sneak into our country from land and sea. Others are temporary workers who overstay their visas and fade into American society. This flies in the face of the fundamental responsibility of the federal government under the Constitution to secure the nation's borders and enforce its immigration laws. Our duty to pay federal income taxes is certainly not optional. Why does our President, so many in our Congress, and the electorate at large seem to feel and act as if the federal government has an option in deciding whether to secure the borders of the country?

Our elected officials and public and private institutions all have an undeniable responsibility in this matter. No ifs, ands, or buts! Outrageously, we have people in our Congress—like House Speaker Nancy Pelosi, liberal Democrat from California (the state suffering most from the flood of illegal aliens)—expressing sympathy with those who are here illegally, by stating that our laws in that regard are "unfair" and that it would be un-American to deport them. She should be forced to read Thomas Jefferson's view of the law at the beginning of this chapter. If our government officials do not respect the rule of law, why should its citizens? What chance does our country have of remaining free and prosperous with a government that willfully ignores its constitutional duties?

The numbers are staggering and discouraging. The Center for Immigration Studies estimates that nearly 12 million illegal immigrants are living in the United States.[2] Their number was estimated to be growing at more than four hundred thousand each year as recently as 2007.[3] The broad range in the numbers reflects how little we really know about the scope of the problem. While most of the public's attention has been focused on illegal aliens from Latin America (some 61 percent come from Mexico[4]), thousands of others are entering each year through our port cities along the east and west coasts and across the Canadian border, from a wide variety of countries in Asia, Africa, and Europe. How many of these might be terrorists planning great harm to our citizens? Nobody knows.

While the number of legal immigrants to the U.S. has changed little since the eighties, the illegal population has risen dramatically, surpassing the number of those entering legally by the mid-nineties. In 2007, the share of our population who are foreign born reached almost one in three.[5]

While many of our lawmakers, corporate leaders, and others ignore or shrug off the influx of illegal aliens, the social costs are extremely high. According to the Federation for American Immigration Reform in 2006, the cost of the illegal population is $36 billion for education, medical care, and incarceration.[6] Despite the claim that illegals are doing the jobs that Americans will not, it is obvious that our citizens who are already filling low-wage jobs are being displaced by those willing to work at even lower wages. Research has indicated that there is a major distribution of wealth away from unskilled American workers to American employers who are using illegal immigrants. While these employers reap the benefits, the taxpayers are left to pay the infrastructure and social costs.

To compound the problem, a large proportion of the wages earned by illegals is never taxed, nor does it otherwise find its way into the U.S. economy. In part, this is because much of the income is never reported to the U.S. taxing authorities. More importantly, earning of illegal immigrants form a large revenue stream out of the U.S. and back to the respective native countries. That amount was estimated to be $23 billion per year back to Mexico along.[7] Repatriation of income earned in the U.S. by Mexican nationals is one of that country's largest revenue streams, hence the incentive Mexican authorities have to turn a blind eye to the illegal migration matter.

A review of the federal government's efforts to address this situation in recent years makes for depressing reading. In 2001, following the election of a Republican Congress and president, a growing number of our citizens—and virtually all conservatives, Republicans, and independents—began to call loudly for an end to this growing crisis by enforcing existing laws designed to gain control of our borders. There finally seemed to be some recognition that our borders were wide open to illegal entry. Then, when the 9/11 disaster opened the public's eyes to the potential for terrorist entry across these same borders, the prospect for meaningful action seemed assured. Astoundingly, instead of responding to the public outcry (which polls suggested included a solid majority of our citizens), President Bush and the Republican Congress took no effective action for six more years and the crisis grew worse.

As more and more Americans were victimized by violent crimes at the hands of illegal immigrants, as emergency rooms were overrun by non-citizens, and as costs skyrocketed for community social services being given to millions of illegal immigrants, grass-roots Republicans and other citizens could only shake their heads in disbelief. How could a Republican President and congressional Republicans ignore their constitutional duty to protect the sovereignty of our nation, particularly when such action was so politically popular with the vast majority of the Republican Party?

When something makes no sense, a good guiding principle is to follow the money: the U.S. Chamber of Commerce for years has heavily funded Republican incumbents and has been adamantly opposed to ending illegal immigration. Their concern has not been for the welfare of legal American citizens but solely for big business, including the construction, agricultural, and service industries, which all benefit from having in place a workforce comprised of individuals who will work for the lowest wages, claim no employment benefits, and keep their mouths shut about working conditions. It is Joe Taxpayer who must then pick up the costs. This outrage is, of course, not just the doing of the Republicans. On the other side of the aisle are the Democrats who, when they see an illegal immigrant, they see a potential new vote for their party. There is shame enough to go around.

Since we now have a 10-percent-plus and rising unemployment rate and have lost millions of jobs since our recession began in 2007, you would think that President Obama would ensure that people here illegally were not taking American jobs. But look at what happened in the $787 billion "stimulus" jobs bill passed by Congress in early 2009. Through it, taxpayer dollars are (we hope) being used to create some two million new temporary jobs, mostly in construction. It is expected that some few hundred thousand of these construction jobs, maybe as many as one in six, will go to illegal immigrants. To avoid this, an amendment to the bill was introduced, largely by Republican members, requiring employers to certify the immigration status of prospective new hires. This would utilize a Department of Homeland Security program called E-Verify, which allows employers to check the validity of Social Security numbers provided by those seeking employment. The program has been judged to be 99 percent successful in identifying those with legal status, but the problem is that the program has been voluntary in nature. However, the U.S. Chamber of Commerce—ever concerned with getting the cheapest labor pool available, regardless of the cost to the nation—fought aggressively against this amendment and (with the help of Democrats with visions of votes in their heads) managed to defeat it. So now, we taxpayers will be paying the salaries and benefits for three hundred thousand illegal immigrants who will be employed under the "stimulus" bill. Meanwhile, three hundred thousand Americans and their families remain out of work in this terrible recession. Unbelievable!

The U.S. Chamber, along with other business groups, also successfully challenged President Bush's regulation, scheduled to go into effect at the beginning of 2009 that would require companies receiving federal contracts of one hundred thousand dollars or more to use E-Verify to confirm the eligibility of its workers. The Chamber, clearly, is no friend of conservatives, the rule of law or the Founders' values, nor is it looking out for the best interest of American citizens. Additionally, it continues to support an array of incompetent career politicians in Washington that do the Chamber's bidding. Very few conservatives are aware of, or will admit, the damage this group is doing to the pursuit of conservative ideals and how it uses its money and power to prevent conservatives from challenging big government, incumbent Republicans. In the battle between conservatives and career politicians with no values, it is important for you to know where this powerful special interest group and its big business allies stand.

No one is a bigger fan of business than I, and I am actively involved in several local chambers of commerce groups that do great work and really help small business owners succeed. However, in a Republican primary I would vote almost every time against the candidate the U.S. Chamber of Commerce is supporting (who will

be the incumbent 99.9 percent of the time) because of the importance of this issue.

Republican politicians often pretend to be outraged about the
illegal immigration crisis but, all the while, do nothing on this
issue. They know that big business money and the U.S. Chamber
support is more important to their campaigns than taking any
action against illegal immigration. They know these hundreds of
thousands of dollars raised by big-business political-action committees (PACs) prevent any primary challengers from being able to
raise enough money to oust them in a primary contest because
individuals do not typically contribute to congressional campaigns.
They also know Republican voters will not vote for a pro-illegal
immigration Democrat, so they get a "free pass" on the issue. In
summary, these politicians do not really have to do anything about
illegal immigration except make comforting statements of understanding to their constituents who care about the issue and just
wait to be re-elected.

In 2007, President Bush called on Congress to endorse a guest-
worker program, stating that immigrants here illegally were taking
jobs that Americans will not take. At that point, both parties,
desperate to appear as though they were doing something about
the crisis, came up with a bill that would have provided a path to
citizenship for illegal immigrants. Americans wisely saw this as an
amnesty bill that would reward illegal behavior while doing nothing
to alter the flood of illegal immigration (except to quicken it). They
viewed this as a congressional scam and charade, recognizing that if
the government will not follow and enforce the laws already on the
books, why should they believe the government would enforce new
immigration laws? As Jefferson observed, if you do not enforce the
laws you have, it really does not matter what the laws say.

Fortunately, this ill-advised amnesty bill was defeated because of
the will of the people. They saw what Congress still refuses to see.
Amnesty undermines U.S. law and our sovereignty, rewards illegal
conduct, costs taxpayers billions, increases crime rates and gang

activity, threatens our national security, and is unfair to the millions of immigrants who follow the law and are awaiting legal entry into the United States. It is worth recalling that, in the eighties, almost three million illegal aliens were granted amnesty by which they were accorded legal status—and their numbers only grew larger.[8]

Unfortunately, President Obama seems determined to resurrect this bill, or a similar version, and it stands a much better chance of passing now that Democrats are totally in control of Congress. If ever there was a cause and a time to protest and march on Capitol Hill, this is it. If an amnesty bill passes, there will be 15 million new democratic voters who will be voting for socialism and more government handouts—and conservatives likely will remain the congressional minority and therefore powerless for generations to come. America will never be the same.

What can we do to get a handle on this problem? I believe in a strategy of attrition through enforcement, designed to remove the economic incentives for illegal immigration. This approach is practical and politically tenable. Although it will sound cold to some, for the economic well-being, quality of life, and security of Americans here legally, and to protect the rule of law, our country must be less hospitable to those who would come here through the breaking of our laws.

Let's look at four measures I believe will create a healthy immigration process, one that will preserve our rule of law, our sovereignty, and our national identity, while allowing a healthy, orderly flow of legal immigrants to enter our country to achieve their dreams and help America prosper:

BOLSTER BORDER SECURITY

First, we need to make sure the crisis does not continue to worsen. This is why we need to ensure total funding for the already-approved-but-slow-on-delivery 854-mile fence along the southern border, as required by federal law, to ensure its expeditious completion and then extend it as needed. Further, the number of border-patrol agents should be increased substantially, by at least twenty-five thousand agents, augmented as necessary by other local, state, and federal resources to prevent any further illegal entry. Additional advanced detection technologies should be employed. We must similarly step up our surveillance and enforcement efforts along our northern border and in our ports.

REQUIRE COMPLIANCE BY EMPLOYERS

We can greatly reduce the number of people entering the country illegally by vigorous enforcement of already existing laws that forbid employers from hiring undocumented alien workers. Once again, we have individuals, this time American employers, breaking U.S. laws with impunity, while members of Congress, labor unions, and others close their eyes. Without these employment opportunities, fewer illegal aliens would enter our country, while millions already here would return home.

We are, however, headed in exactly the wrong direction. Between 1999 and 2003, the U.S. Immigration and Customs Enforcement (ICE) operations focused on employers was actually scaled back 95 percent and the number of fines collected from employers decreased from $3.6 million to $212,000 during that period. Incredibly, while in 1999 the United States government initiated fines against 417 companies, in 2004 fines were levied against a grand total of three employers![9]

There is no excuse for employers to flout U.S. law. They have at their disposal a powerful and very inexpensive tool to establish the immigration status of jobseekers and their workers, if they choose to use it (and most, clearly, do not). As mentioned previously, this is the Department of Homeland Security's electronic database, the E-Verify system, which an employer can use to confirm that a prospective employee is authorized to work in the U.S. Again, its success rate is 99 percent and thirteen states now require its use, but its application is still very limited around the nation. This should be changed through federal legislation that would require all employers to apply the E-Verify system in all hiring situations. Moreover, employers should be required to send in their employees' names and Social Security numbers if they are going to deduct the employee's wages on their income tax returns.

Irrespective of other changes in our system, employers must be held responsible for the health care costs of any of their illegal aliens or guest workers. Such a policy would dramatically increase the real cost of employing illegals and, consequently, help put an end to this hiring practice carried out at the expense of tax-paying American workers. As it stands now, employers get cheap labor while taxpayers are stuck paying for the health care costs and other government benefits being extended to individuals who are in the country illegally and breaking our laws. Outrageous!

IMPROVE THE LEGAL IMMIGRATION PROCESS

At the same time, we must reduce the backlogs and streamline the whole process for immigrant jobseekers and employers who want to follow the law. We must also simplify and expedite the application processes for temporary visas. This can be accomplished by hiring more personnel at the U.S. Citizenship and Immigration Services and the FBI. Caps on numbers of all categories of temporary worker visas granted each year can be increased as appropriate, but only if it is demonstrated that there are no Americans capable and willing to do the jobs.

ENGLISH AS AN OFFICIAL LANGUAGE

We must also insist that English be the language of use in the schools and government settings, except for remedial English and second-language courses. Giving immigrants the easy way out by providing documentation in other languages than English is doing them no favors. A national language is a unifying force and a powerful catalyst for assimilating individuals into American society.

The fact that our Census Bureau is preparing to release documentation for the forthcoming census in *fifty* languages is an abomination, even beyond the expense involved. How many of us would expect that if we were to move to France or Spain or any other non-English-speaking country in the world, the government there would provide us with English translations of government documents? Immigrants to our shores should not expect it either. The quicker they learn our language, the better off we all will be.

CONCLUSION

It is not the critic who counts: not the man who points out how the strong man stumbles or where the doer of deeds could have done better. The credit belongs to the man who is actually in the arena, whose face is marred by dust and sweat and blood, who strives valiantly, who errs and comes up short again and again, because there is no effort without error or shortcoming, but who knows the great enthusiasms, the great devotions, who spends himself for a worthy cause; who, at the best, knows, in the end, the triumph of high achievement, and who, at the worst, if he fails, at least he fails while daring greatly, so that his place shall never be with those cold and timid souls who knew neither victory nor defeat.

—President Theodore Roosevelt,
"Citizenship in a Republic" Speech at the Sorbonne,
April 23, 1910[1]

I HOPE THIS BOOK encourages you to respond to the great challenges of our day with that same fighting spirit.

None of the changes necessary to place this nation back on the correct course will happen unless many more of our citizens are motivated to become aggressively and passionately involved in fighting for our Founders' beliefs and values. The trend in recent years seems to be in the other direction, with a largely uninformed, apathetic public being led by a multitude of career politicians who do not solve problems but, instead, make them worse. As our Founders knew, however, with God on our side, anything is possible. He will do the heavy lifting and the miraculous. We just need to do our part.

I hope that many will read and enjoy this book and in the process gain a better understanding of our Founders' timeless principles and become inspired to fight for solutions to the nation's challenges based on these principles. Mostly, however, I have written this book for my young children, Noah and Natalia. I want them to understand and appreciate the rich heritage bequeathed them by their Founding Fathers. I hope to inspire them to extend their legacy. I want them to be armed with timeless principles and effective solutions to America's challenges. Finally, I want them also to share my sense of concern that these values—conservative values—are being threatened by both external and internal forces.

My concern is that unless we, the standard-bearers of conservatism, can re-instill into America the principles and values embraced by our Founders, our children's future will be mortgaged through crushing debt, an oppressive central government, loss of personal freedom, and an apathetic, overly dependent citizenry.

It need not turn out that way. Our recent past does not have to be prologue. Despite the media's preoccupation with bad news, my own recent experiences and readings convince me that there is a solid core of Americans who feel as I do, optimistic about the unrealized potential of this country. There are, however, too many of our citizens who have become cynical about government in general, others too absorbed in the trivial matters of the day, and some just too lazy to become involved. Regardless, this silent majority can—*must*—be mobilized if conservatives are to recover the ground they have ceded to liberals over the last two decades.

There are no simple answers to today's challenges. To quote President Reagan again, "There are no easy answers, but there are simple answers. We must have the courage to do what we know is morally right."[2] The "Conservative Comeback" must begin with a refocused, renewed, and reenergized Republican Party, driven by new and vigorous leadership. It is all too clear that the present leadership is too identified across the political spectrum as incompetent and filled with a lust for power and a preoccupation with staying in office.

The "Conservative Comeback" must be focused on wealth creation, balanced budgets, states' rights, the rule of law, and our

Constitution. These are politically winning issues and represent distinct differences with the liberal Democratic viewpoint.

Today we are too dependent on an inefficient, often corrupt federal government. The bad news is that, to turn this around, there will have to be short-term pain and lifestyle adjustments for the long-term well being of our country. Those are the facts our politicians dare not tell you. Instead, they keep trying for quick fixes to avoid any pain, which merely compounds our problems.

———

I have a dream and a vision that in four years our next president will send this message in his/her inaugural address:

My fellow Americans:

We have a wonderful Constitution. It was handed down to us by our Forefathers and has, for 230 years, established this nation as the greatest in the world. It secures our freedom and protects our God-given rights.

Slowly, over the years, we have lost sight of this heritage and our country is suffering from it. While the Founding Fathers went to great lengths to ensure that the power remained with the citizens and that the role of the federal government would be severely limited, Washington has now taken on a dominant role in the lives of our citizens and is destroying our freedom. Too many responsibilities have been shifted to Washington and away from the local and state level where they can be discharged more effectively and efficiently. We have created a system of dependency on the federal government that is eroding the spirit of independence, self-sacrifice, and self-worth that made America so productive and vital over the decades.

My fellow citizens, we are going to once again honor the Constitution and our Declaration of Independence by working to re-establish their time-honored values and principles. This will require commitment, sacrifice, and hard work from all of us.

In setting our course for the next four years, my administration will focus its efforts on strengthening the government's performance in those critical areas where the federal government has a clear and essential mandate from our Constitution.

This begins with national defense. My overriding job is to keep you all safe. This involves ensuring that our nation's military capability remains second to none in the world; it means conducting a foreign policy based on mutual respect for others nations, but one that does not shy away from taking forceful, decisive action when threatened; and it means keeping our borders closed to illegal entry and ending illegal immigration, once and for all!

We must also get our financial house in order. I will work to ensure that more of your tax dollars stay at home, in your states and your localities, instead of being trans-ferred inefficiently to Washington and then back again. States' rights and the Tenth Amendment will be honored and unconstitutional earmarks will be eliminated.

Further, I pledge my commitment to balancing the federal budget and ensuring that it stays balanced. Following the example of many of our states, I will work for an amendment to the Constitution that requires the budget to be balanced on an annual basis. We can no longer mortgage the future of this nation and our children's future to the mountain of debt we have been irresponsibly building up.

The goals of reducing the federal budget deficit and limiting the role of the federal government go hand in hand. Many federal programs will be eliminated or cut. We will also overhaul our major entitlement programs,

Social Security and Medicare. To preserve them in a manner that meets the needs of our people without bankrupting the nation, it will be necessary to increase age and eligibility requirements. At the same time, the federal government's raid on your Social Security contributions will end, once and for all!

We will also move to drastically lower health care costs by producing a nation of healthier people, beginning with our children, who, once again, will have mandatory physical fitness and healthier food in their schools. This, however, is a proper role for our states and local communities; and I will work to return the responsibility for taking care of people's needs closer to where they live.

To revitalize our economy, I will work with our Congress to get rid of our current tax system and replace it with a much simpler and equitable Fair Tax. This will promote wealth-creation and bring an avalanche of new business and employment opportunities for all citizens, while significantly increasing Americans' standard of living.

And we will, once and for all, do away with our complex, incomprehensible tax code, and also the IRS as you know it. These ninety thousand pages of rules and regulations have become a blight on our economy and the democratic process. As it exists today, the tax code penalizes productivity, confuses and frustrates the average taxpayer, allows an underground economy and illegal immigrants to escape paying taxes and helps career politicians in Washington abuse their power.

Beyond national defense, balancing budgets and tax reform, the federal government can, and must, play central roles in several other key program areas. One of these is energy policy. Our oil-based economy is too vulnerable to the whims and policies of other nations. We will immediately put in place a comprehensive energy policy that sets out a vision and pathway toward energy independence for this Nation. This must promote development of a broad array of domestic energy sources, as well as new technologies, and with a much greater utilization of nuclear energy, natural gas, and renewable sources such as wind, solar and biomass.

Ultimately, the fate of our nation's economy, its security, its quality of life and its opportunities rests in your hands. The choices you make—in the voting booth, at work, around the dinner table, and in your personal life—are what will determine whether we prosper and grow as a nation and whether your children, and theirs, will have the same opportunities and freedoms with which we have been blessed. This will require a change of mindset by many in our population today who have come to expect more from their government in Washington than from themselves. It will require all of you to hold your public servants to high standards of performance and personal conduct, and it will necessitate a rebirth of patriotism and pride in our country.

My fellow Americans, I have laid out a broad agenda of challenging tasks to ensure that this nation remains true to the beliefs and callings of our Founders. If we rise to the challenges, we can go forward in this new century confident that our basic freedoms will endure, that America's position in the world remains second to none, and that a renewed spirit of hope, optimism, and excitement pervades our lives. The tasks that confront us are numerous and difficult, but with all of us committed and pulling together, success is assured.

Thank you, God bless you, and may God bless America.

In these uncertain times, America needs a strong "Conservative Comeback," and our Founding Fathers can show us the way.

Appendix

My Run for Congress and What I Learned

In December, 2006, I announced my candidacy for the congressional seat in the Eighth District of Florida. I had three motivations. The first was that over the previous decade, I had become increasingly disillusioned by the direction our nation was heading on an array of economic and social problems and especially by the absence of effective leadership from congressional conservatives and Republicans. Second, I believed I had good solutions to our national challenges and would do a very good job if elected. Third, I learned from my call-in radio show, *A Different Direction*, that many shared my views and were equally put off by the abysmal performance by the incumbent in the seat, Republican Ric Keller.

I had no illusions that the road to Washington would be easy. I had never run for public office before nor did I have connections to political insiders, local officials or special-interest groups. Being a personal-injury attorney, my profession did not endear me to a lot of Republicans and, in fact, disqualified me immediately in some circles.

On the other hand, I saw two important benefits from a quest for public office, regardless of whether I ultimately won or not. Since my radio show was based on the proposition that, "If you don't like what's going on, don't just complain, propose a solution," I felt that I should walk the walk by putting into practice what I was challenging my listeners to do. Thus, just making the effort to effect change was appealing to me. Further, campaigning for office would provide special opportunities to share with others my vision and ideas on how to restore conservative values and principles in American politics. I believed that I had well-thought-out ideas and proposals that deserved to be heard and to be given a chance to succeed. Since I was in a position financially to run for office and to leave my career for two-plus years, I was the last one who should be sitting on the sidelines complaining about an incompetent Congress.

Just a cursory look at the prospects of winning the election was sobering. Since 1982, only four congressional incumbents in Florida had been defeated, including in both primary and general elections. Think about that. We have 25 congressional districts in the state, each with two races per election held every two years. Thus, over a twenty-six-year period and 650 races, incumbents won 99.3 percent of the time! That is a terrible indictment of our political system and, ultimately, we, the voting public.

That said, I felt that the incumbent in my district was vulnerable. Keller epitomized for me what I thought was wrong with our Congress and my Republican Party. For four terms (eight years), he had been virtually silent on many of the most challenging issues facing the nation, including our energy crisis and health care reform. He voted billions and billions of dollars for earmarks, farm subsidies, and other government programs that were bankrupting the country, all the while claiming to be a conservative. I especially objected to Keller's voting against the troop surge in Iraq, an expression of defeatism that would damage our troops' morale and encourage the enemy. Further, his intention to run for a fifth term in the Congress broke a term-limit pledge he had made previously to the voters of the district. Breaking that commitment was, in my view, incredibly abusive to those who provided him with support for his previous run for office. It is an act that greatly diminishes the respect that people have for our elected officials and the Republican Party.

So, with this as the backdrop, I launched my run. My campaign managers, Jeremy Hill and Rosa Alvarez, worked with me for two years, sometimes around the clock, fighting against both the political establishment and the apathy of many potential voters. Pointing to the Republican primary in August 2008, we attended as many

Republican, Rotary, Kiwanis Club, and other group meetings as we could identify, where I would give presentations on such topics as the state of our economy and the national debt crisis. We held numerous town hall meetings, small meet-and-greet events, and fundraisers where we raised only a few thousand dollars at a time.

I met pastors throughout the district, held a pastor's breakfast, and my wife, Ninette, and my family visited different churches every Sunday, as well as Bible study sessions on Wednesdays. As a family, we also participated in parades on holidays, set up booths at art festivals, and attended a host of other community events and galas for various charities. If there was a Republican event, we were there. If there was a community event, we were there, shaking hands and talking to anyone and everyone we could about the campaign and the issues that we deemed important for our district and for the nation. I quickly developed an appreciation for the rigors of running for public office, but also the joys, too. Most gratifying was the hard work and determined effort of my small, paid staff (who now are lifelong friends) and the many volunteers who worked so hard for me. I will always be so thankful to all of them.

Getting the message out, whether via mailings, billboards, radio, or TV is very expensive. For a first-timer with no political or special-interest connections, getting financial backing is daunting. As it turned out, I invested $275,000 of my own funds in the campaign, and we raised another $130,000 from individuals, most of whom had never contributed to a congressional campaign before. A major disadvantage any newcomer faces is that the national, state, and district political parties line up almost automatically behind the party incumbent, no matter how he or she has performed.

Consequently, I found myself being outspent by my opponent by a considerable amount. It was a continuous struggle to reach potential voters and to gain the 4,300 signatures needed on a petition required to get my name on the ballot. Supported by a few additional staff I was able to hire, we began to walk the district house to house. Since my district includes parts of four counties (Orange,

Lake, Marion, and a small part of Osceola), our small team logged many, many miles. We tried hard to debate the incumbent, but he skipped even those that had been scheduled by various local groups and the media, except for one without an audience. (That debate can be seen on the Web site: www.toddlongforCongress.com.)

In the end, I lost the primary election, but was greatly comforted in the close count: 20,350 votes for me, 22,000 for the incumbent. The end result is that we now have ultraliberal Democrat Alan Grayson, who went on to defeat Keller, representing us in a district that heretofore was represented by a Republican.

Along the way, I discovered the following that I believe important to anyone else who wishes to take the journey:

1. Our republic works: while imperfect, certainly, our democratic system of government provides every citizen with the right and the opportunity to run for public office, to say whatever he or she wants to during the campaign, and to have a chance of being elected by fellow citizens through a secret ballot. Few people in the world can claim this privilege.

2. Money talks: campaign financing and the dominant role of special-interest money is the biggest flaw in the system. Candidates who have the largest "war chest" funded by various special-interest groups win virtually every national race, as lesser-endowed competitors have difficulty in getting the necessary exposure to the electorate. We must have term limits to help decentralize our federal government and have a continuous flow of new voices and new ideas lead this nation.

3. Hard to reach voters: one obstacle for me was the difficulty in reaching senior citizens in apartments with "no soliciting" restrictions and families living in gated communities. I did not realize how many voters can

only be reached through big money by way of TV or radio advertising.

4. Take the high road: I was most proud of the fact that I stuck to the issues and avoided personal attacks on my opponent, apart from his voting record. On the other hand, not once in the campaign did he criticize my policies or proposals. When the polls showed a tight race, he sent a personal attack mail piece to district voters, which had nothing to do with the issues. Perhaps this had some bearing on the outcome. The irony is that Ric Keller's democratic opponent in the general election did the same thing to him, with devastating results. Regardless, a true statesmen should not go down that road. One can only hope and pray that the voters will begin to reject candidates who use personal attacks as their modus operandi. Obviously, if candidates had good solutions to our problems, they would be touting those solutions instead of engaging in character attacks. If we voters continue to reward these character assassins with election victories, we should not be surprised if we have an incompetent, self-serving Congress. The blame is on us.

5. Voter cynicism: I discovered along the way widespread disillusionment with the government in Washington, especially with the Congress, and deep disappointment with the performance of the Republican leadership. Many questioned the value of voting when everything seemed to be locked up in favor of incumbents. Others felt that their opinion on matters of state did not matter; they are either neglected or ignored by their representatives, whom they rarely hear from except at election time. Clearly, this downward spiral in the political process must be stopped and reversed if our

democratic Republic is to be meaningful to American citizens and enduring for the nation.

6. The people care: despite the cynicism, I came away from the campaign encouraged and uplifted by the thousands of thoughtful, interested, knowledgeable, and decent people I encountered. They all reflected a deep love of family, country, and God that would have made our Founding Fathers think that it was worthwhile. They yearn for a return to the values that made this country so strong and envied; values that I feel are the essence of conservatism.

These days one can easily come away from reading the papers or watching the TV thinking that the whole world has gone mad; that decency, honesty, and intelligence are nowhere to be found. My journey showed me just how far that view is from reality in our land. In the final analysis, it was this discovery that made the journey so worthwhile and the continued fight so necessary.

Notes

Introduction

1. Jonah Goldberg, "What the GOP can learn from a pizza chain," http://article.nationalreview.com/?q=OGJkNjhjZWFmYmYwODA0ZjZmZWE1N2FmNmE4ZWIwNGE=, January 8, 2010.
2. Web site: http://www.twainquotes.com/Death.html (accessed January 4, 2010).
3. Larry Kudlow, "What Did Reagan's Inaugural Say?" http://article.nationalreview.com/383308/what-did-reagans-inaugural-say/larry-kudlow, January 19, 2009.
4. Web site: http://archives.cnn.com/2002/ALLPOLITICS/05/13/farm.bill/ (accessed January 4, 2010).
5. Web site: http://www.brainyquote.com/quotes/quotes/r/ronaldreag183750.html (accessed January 4, 2010).

★ Part I: America's Changing Values

Chapter 1 The Wisdom of Our Founding Fathers

1. Web site: http://www.reagan.utexas.edu/archives/speeches/1988/080888b.htm (accessed January 4, 2010).
2. Web site: http://www.dartmouth.edu/~dwebster/speeches/bunker-hill.html (accessed January 4, 2010).
3. Web site: http://www.bartleby.com/73/1593.html (accessed January 4, 2010).
4. Web site: http://www.ushistory.org/PAINE/crisis/c-01.htm (accessed January 4, 2010).
5. Larry Schweikart, "Did You Know that Half the Declaration's Signers Had Divinity School Training?", http://www.freerepublic.com/focus/f-news/1413314/posts, May 30, 2005.
6. Web site: http://www.britannica.com/bps/additionalcontent/18/24418662/THE-RISE-AND-FALL-OF-SCHOOL-VOUCHERS-A-STORY-OF-RELIGION-RACE-AND-POLITICS (accessed January 4, 2010).
7. Web site: http://thinkexist.com/quotation/our_constitution_was_made_only_for_a_moral_and/262425.html (accessed January 4, 2010).
8. Web site: http://www.goodreads.com/author/quotes/63859.James_Madison (accessed January 4, 2010).
9. Web site: http://www.wnd.com/index.php?fa=PAGE.view&pageId=67735 (accessed January 4, 2010).

Chapter 2 Abandoning Our Heritage

1. Barry Goldwater, *The Conscience of a Conservative* (Washington, D.C.: Regnery Publishing, Inc., 1994).

2. Barack Obama, *The Audacity of Hope* (New York: Crown Publishers, 2006).

3. Web site: http://article.nationalreview.com/?q=YmMzMDczNzBhMjZhMjh lZmYzYzI3ZTYwNzVhZTNjNTM= (accessed January 4, 2010).

4. Jerry Tuma, *From Boom to Bust and Beyond* (Lake Mary, FL: Excel Books, 2009), 136.

5. F.A. Hayek, *The Constitution of Liberty* (Chicago: University of Chicago Press, 1960).

6. Dan Walters, "Debt may be half a trillion dollars," *Sacramento Bee*, Nov. 29, 2009.

7. Dennis Cauchon, "Benefit spending soars to new high," *USA Today*, June 4, 2009.

Chapter 3 Conservatism vs. Dependency

1. Goldwater, *The Conscience of a Conservative*.

2. Senator John McCain, speech to GOPAC, November 16, 2006, http://www.presidency.ucsb.edu/ws/index.php?pid=77147 (accessed January 4, 2010).

3. Web site: http://www.whitehouse.gov/the_press_office/Remarks-by-the -President-at-Fort-Myers-Town-Hall/ (accessed January 4, 2010).

4. Goldwater, *The Conscience of a Conservative*.

5. Leslie Wayne, "Obama's tax returns," *New York Times*, March 26, 2008.

6. Ibid.

7. Matt Kelley, "Biden gave average of $369 to charity a year," *USA Today*, September 12, 2008.

8. Web site: http://article.nationalreview.com/?q=OTZiY2EyNjllZmI3MjBiO DdiM2ViNjc5ZmYxNjI1Zjg= (accessed January 4, 2010).

9. Web site: http://www.philanthropy.iupui.edu/Research2007.pdf (accessed January 4, 2010).

10. Scott A. Hodge, "Number of Americans Outside the Income Tax System Continues to Grow," www.taxfoundation.org, June 9, 2005.

11. Web site: http://www.lewrockwell.com/paul/paul109.html (accessed January 4, 2010).

Chapter 4 Re-establishing the Founders' Values

1. Thomas W. Evans, *The Education of Ronald Reagan: The General Electric Years and the Untold Story of His Conversion to Conservatism* (New York: Columbia University Press, 2008).

2. Web site: http://www.christianitytoday.com/holidays/memorial/features/ 33h010.html (accessed January 4, 2010).

3. Web site: http://my.barackobama.com/page/community/post/stateupdates/ gGg2xq (accessed January 4, 2010).

4. Megan O'Matz, "Governor Crist and entourage traveled in style across Europe as businesses and taxpayers footed the bill," http://www .sun-sentinel.com/news/nationworld/sfl-flgovtrip07sbdec07,0,5721620.story, December 7, 2008.

5. Web site: http://www.brainyquote.com/quotes/quotes/r/ronaldreag124946 .html (accessed January 4, 2010).

6. Web site: http://www.groveatlantic.com/grove/bin/wc.dll?groveproc~genauth ~568~1048~EXCERPT (accessed January 4, 2010).

⭐ PART II: PUTTING AMERICA'S FINANCIAL HOUSE IN ORDER

CHAPTER 5 THE ROAD TO A $12 TRILLION NATIONAL DEBT

1. Joseph Farah, "Why democracy doesn't work," http://www.wnd.com/news/ article.asp?ARTICLE_ID=55401, April 27, 2007.

2. Web site: http://www.brillig.com/debt_clock/ (accessed January 4, 2010).

3. Ibid.

4. Jerome R. Corsi, "Federal obligations exceed world GDP: Does $65.5 trillion terrify anyone yet?" http://www.wnd.com/index.php?pageId=88851, February 13, 2009.

5. Web site: http://www.chrismartenson.com/crashcourse (accessed January 4, 2010).

6. Julie Mason, "Interest payments on national debt set to explode," http:// www.washingtonexaminer.com/politics/Interest-payments-on-national-debt -set-to-explode-8577764-71953337.html, November 24, 2009.

7. Web site: http://www.concordcoalition.org/learn/debt/national-debt (accessed January 4, 2010).

8. Web site: http://www.treasurydirect.gov/govt/reports/pd/histdebt/histdebt_ histo4.htm (accessed January 4, 2010).

9. Ibid.

10. Web site: http://www.treasurydirect.gov/govt/reports/pd/histdebt/histdebt_ histo4.htm (accessed January 4, 2010).

11. Web site: http://www.brillig.com/debt_clock/ (accessed January 4, 2010).

12. Web site: http://www.treasurydirect.gov/govt/reports/pd/histdebt/histdebt_ histo4.htm (accessed January 4, 2010).

13. Web site: http://www.treasurydirect.gov/govt/reports/pd/histdebt/histdebt_ histo5.htm (accessed January 4, 2010).

14. Web site: http://www.heritage.org/research/features/budgetChartbook/ Federal-spending-growing-faster-than-federal-revenue.aspx (accessed January 4, 2010).

15. Web site: http://www.usatoday.com/news/washington/2008-12-15-deficit_ N.htm (accessed January 4, 2010).

16. Lori Montgomery, "Deficit Projected To Swell Beyond Earlier Estimates," http://www.washingtonpost.com/wp-dyn/content/article/2009/03/20/ AR2009032001820.html, March 21, 2009.

17. Web site: http://www.treasurydirect.gov/NP/BPDLogin?application=np (accessed January 4, 2010).

18. Web site: http://www.brillig.com/debt_clock/ (accessed January 4, 2010).

19. Lori Montgomery, "Deficit Projected To Swell Beyond Earlier Estimates," http://www.washingtonpost.com/wp-dyn/content/article/2009/03/20/ AR2009032001820.html, March 21, 2009.

20. Web site: http://www.cbo.gov/ftpdocs/100xx/doc10014/03-20- PresidentBudget.pdf (accessed January 4, 2010).

21. Dennis Cauchon, "States and cities borrow big," http://www.usatoday .com/news/nation/2009-05-03-borrowing_N.htm, May 4, 2009.

22. Web site: http://www.treas.gov/tic/mfh.txt (accessed January 4, 2010).

23. Mark Trumbull, "Post-Depression first: Americans get more money from government than they give back," http://www.csmonitor.com/ Money/2009/1109/post-depression-first-americans-get-more-money-from -government-than-they-give-back, November 9, 2009.

24. Jerome R. Corsi, "Federal obligations exceed world GDP: Does $65.5 trillion terrify anyone yet?" http://www.wnd.com/index.php?pageId=88851, February 13, 2009."

25. Web site: http://constitutionalconservative.wordpress.com/myth-majority -of-federal-budget-is-defense/ (accessed January 4, 2010).

26. U.S. Treasury Department, Treasury Bulletin, December 2008.

27. Web site: http://federalreserve.gov/releases/z1/Current/z1r-2.pdf (accessed January 4, 2010).

CHAPTER 6 A 12-POINT PLAN TO REDUCE GOVERNMENT SPENDING AND BALANCE THE BUDGET

1. Web site: http://etext.virginia.edu/jefferson/quotations/jeff1340.htm (accessed January 4, 2010).

CHAPTER 7 OUR DYSFUNCTIONAL TAX CODE AND THE FAIR-TAX SOLUTION

1. Web site: http://thinkexist.com/quotation/i_predict_future_happiness_for_ americans_if_they/225991.html (accessed January 4, 2010).

2. Web site: http://www.glennbeck.com/content/articles/article/198/22535/ (accessed January 4, 2010).

3. Web site: http://www.ntu.org/main/page.php?PageID=6 (accessed January 4, 2010).

4. Web site: http://www.ntu.org/main/press.php?PressID=1004&org_name=NTU (accessed January 4, 2010).

5. Ibid.

6. Op-Ed, "Geithner's Tax Code: The nominee explains his payment 'mistake.'" http://online.wsj.com/article/SB123258571706004547.html, January 22, 2009.

7. Joel Slemrod, "Cheating Ourselves: The Economics of Tax Evasion," *Journal of Economic Perspectives*, Vol. 21, No. 1, Winter 2007, p. 29.

8. Adam Shell, "Cash of the titans: Criticism of pay for fund execs grows," http://www.usatoday.com/money/companies/management/2007-08-29-private-equity-pay_N.htm, August 29, 2007.

9. Web site: http://www.cus.wayne.edu/content/maps/Det-historical-popdensity.pdf (accessed January 4, 2010).

10. Julianne Pepitone, "Detroit joblessness worst among big cities," http://money.cnn.com/2009/06/30/news/economy/detroit_unemployment_metropolitan_local/index.htm?postversion=2009063012, June 30, 2009.

11. Web site: http://www.brookings.edu/reports/2006/07useconomics_wial.aspx (accessed January 4, 2010).

12. Web site: http://www.ap.com/article/ALeqM5h8juBKyMw6Uz2fTUih5BZYSPJBKwD9CKLU482 (accessed January 4, 2010).

13. Op-Ed, "Millionaires Go Missing: Maryland's fleeced taxpayers fight back," http://online.wsj.com/article/SB124329282377252471.html, May 27, 2009.

14. Web site: http://www.usa-presidents.info/union/kennedy-3.html (accessed January 4, 2010).

15. Web site: http://www.bls.gov/news.release/empsit.nr0.htm (accessed January 4, 2010).

16. Ibid.

17. Web site: http://www.marketwatch.com/story/more-than-8-million-homes-face-foreclosure-in-next-4-years (accessed January 4, 2010).

18. Web site: http://transcripts.cnn.com/TRANSCRIPTS/0711/30/cnr.02.html (accessed January 4, 2010).

19. Web site: http://www.fairtax.org/PDF/FairTaxPrebateExplained2007.pdf (accessed January 4, 2010).

20. Web site: http://quotes.liberty-tree.ca/quote/ronald_reagan_quote_ac1e (accessed January 4, 2010).

CHAPTER 8 PRESIDENT OBAMA'S BIG-GOVERNMENT AGENDA AND RESPONSE TO THE RECESSION

1. Web site: http://www.brainyquote.com/quotes/quotes/w/winstonchu101776. html (accessed January 4, 2010).
2. WSJ Blogs, "Government Bails Out Fannie Mae and Freddie Mac," http:// blogs.wsj.com/developments/2008/09/08/government-bails-out-fannie-mae-and-freddie-mac/, September 8, 2008.
3. Nick Timiraos, "Questions Surround Fannie, Freddie," http://online.wsj. com/article/SB10001424052748704234304574626630520798314.html, December 30, 2009.
4. Web site: http://www.opensecrets.org/news/2008/09/update-fannie-mae-and-freddie.html (accessed January 4, 2010).
5. James R. Hagerty and Jessica Holzer, "U.S. Move to Cover Fannie, Freddie Losses Stirs Controversy," http://online.wsj.com/article/ SB126168307200704747.html, December 28, 2009.
6. Web site: http://www.businessweek.com/news/2010-01-12/u-s-lawmakers-optimistic-gm-chrysler-will-repay-taxpayer-aid.html (accessed January 4, 2010).
7. Web site:http://www.aier.org/research/briefs/1488-tax-revenue-plummets (accessed January 4, 2010).
8. Web site: http://www.cbo.gov/ftpdocs/105xx/doc10521/ 2009BudgetUpdate_Summary.pdf (accessed January 4, 2010).
9. Ibid.

CHAPTER 9 FIGHTING FOR CAPITALISM—WARTS AND ALL

1. Web site: http://quotes.liberty-tree.ca/quotes.nsf/quotes_author!ReadForm& Start=21&Count=20&RestrictToCategory=sir+winston+churchill (accessed January 4, 2010).
2. George Gilder, *Wealth and Poverty* (New York: Basic Books, 1981).
3. Ibid.
4. Ibid.
5. Ibid.
6. Web site: http://thinkexist.com/quotation/within_the_covers_of_the_bible_ are_all_the/337336.html (accessed January 4, 2010).
7. Web site: http://www.cis.org/IllegalImmigration-ShiftingTide (accessed January 4, 2010).

8. Web site: http://www.rasmussenreports.com/public_content/politics/ general_politics/april_2009/just_53_say_capitalism_better_than_socialism (accessed January 4, 2010).

★ PART III: REFORMING OUR INSTITUTIONS

CHAPTER 10 SOLVING OUR EDUCATION CRISIS

1. Web site: http://etext.virginia.edu/jefferson/quotations/jeff1350.htm (accessed January 4, 2010).
2. Web site: http://www.brainyquote.com/quotes/quotes/a/abrahamlin133687.html (accessed January 4, 2010).
3. Web site: http://www.ed.gov/about/overview/fed/10facts/edlite-chart.html (accessed January 4, 2010).
4. Web site: http://eric.ed.gov/ERICWebPortal/custom/portlets/recordDetails/detailmini.jsp?_nfpb=true&_&ERICExtSearch_SearchValue_0=ED507071&ERICExtSearch_SearchType_0=no&accno=ED507071 (accessed January 4, 2010).
5. PISA 2007: OECD Program for International Student Assessment, Paris.
6. PISA 2007: Science Competencies for Tomorrow's World, OECD Program for International Student Assessment, Paris.
7. Ibid.
8. *Understanding High School Graduation Rates: 2009*, Alliance for Excellent Education, Washington, D.C.
9. Gary Davis, "The High School Dropout's Economic Ripple Effect," http://online.wsj.com/article/SB122455013168452477.html (accessed January 4, 2010).
10. Ibid.
11. Ibid.
12. Web site: http://www.newhorizons.org/strategies/multicultural/le.htm (accessed January 4, 2010).
13. Web site: http://www2.prnewswire.com/cgi-bin/stories.pl?ACCT=104&STORY=/www/story/09-26-2006/0004440118&EDATE (accessed January 4, 2010).
14. Ibid.
15. Web site: http://alumni.unc.edu/article.aspx?sid=6660 (accessed January 4, 2010).
16. Web site: http://www2.prnewswire.com/cgi-bin/stories.pl?ACCT=104&STORY=/www/story/09-26-2006/0004440118&EDATE (accessed January 4, 2010).

17. Rob Stein and Donna St. George, "Number of Unwed Mothers Has Risen Sharply in U.S., Women in 20s, 30s Are Driving Trend, Report Shows," http://www.washingtonpost.com/wp-dyn/content/article/2009/05/13/AR2009051301628.html, May 14, 2009.

18. Web site: http://www.heritage.org/research/features/Issues/issuearea/Budget.cfm (accessed January 4, 2010).

CHAPTER 11 CHRISTIANS ARISE AND FIGHT FOR AMERICA: THE ROLE OF THE CHURCH

1. Web site: http://thinkexist.com/quotation/are_you_willing_to_spend_time_studying_the_issues/338212.html (accessed January 4, 2010).

2. *Church of the Holy Trinity v. United States*, 143 U.S. 457 (1892).

3. Ibid.

4. *United States v. Macintosh*, 283 U.S. 605 (1931).

5. *Everson v. Board of Education*, 330 U. S. 1 (1947).

6. Web site: http://www.cdc.gov/nchs/fastats/divorce.htm (accessed January 4, 2010).

7. Web site: http://www.cdc.gov/nchs/pressroom/09newsreleases/unmarriedbirths.htm (accessed January 4, 2010).

CHAPTER 12 THE U.S. SUPREME COURT'S LEADING ROLE IN AMERICA'S DECLINE

1. Web site: http://www.gutenberg.org/dirs/etext90/linc111h.htm (accessed January 4, 2010).

2. Web site: http://www.usgovernmentspending.com/usgs_line.php?title= (accessed January 4, 2010).

3. Web site: http://www.whitehouse.gov/omb/budget/fy2010/assets/hist01z1.xls (accessed January 4, 2010).

4. Web site: http://www.humanevents.com/article.php?id=31343 (accessed January 4, 2010).

5. Web site: http://www2.census.gov/govs/apes/08fedfun.pdf (accessed January 4, 2010).

6. Goldwater, *Conscience of a Conservative*.

7. Web site: http://topics.law.cornell.edu/constitution/articlei (accessed January 4, 2010).

8. Ibid.

9. Web site: http://topics.law.cornell.edu/constitution/billofrights (accessed January 4, 2010).

10. *United States v. Butler*, 297 U. S. 1 (1936).

11. *Helvering v. Davis*, 301 U.S. 619 (1937).

12. Kathy Kiely, "Some states pass sovereignty measures," http://www
    .usatoday.com/news/nation/2009-05-14-secede_N.htm, May 17, 2009.
13. Web site: http://topics.law.cornell.edu/constitution/articlevi (accessed
    January 4, 2010).
14. Web site: http://topics.law.cornell.edu/constitution/billofrights (accessed
    January 4, 2010).
15. David Barton, *Original Intent* (Aledo, TX: 2000).

CHAPTER 13 DISMANTLING CONGRESS'S
INCUMBENCY PROTECTION PROGRAM

1. Web site: http://thinkexist.com/quotation/concentrated_power_has_always_
   been_the_enemy_of/223542.html (accessed January 4, 2010).
2. Web site: http://www.notable-quotes.com/r/reagan_ronald.html (accessed
   January 4, 2010).
3. Brody Mullins And T.W. Farnam, "Recession Thinned Ranks of
   Washington Lobbyists Last Year," htttp://online.wsj.com/article/
   SB123682079838603285.html, March 12, 2009.
4. Jeffrey H. Birnbaum, "Officials Fail To Track Lobbying, Report Says,"
   http://www.washingtonpost.com/wp-dyn/articles/A35425-2005Apr7.html,
   April 8, 2005.
5. Web site: http://www.opensecrets.org/revolving/top.php?display=M
   (accessed January 4, 2010).
6. Web site: http://www.opensecrets.org/bigpicture/reelect.php (accessed
   January 4, 2010).
7. Web site: http://election.dos.state.fl.us/elections/resultsarchive/TurnoutRpt
   .asp?ElectionDate=11/4/2008&DATAMODE= (accessed January 4, 2010).
8. Paul Kane and Scott Wilson, "Obama Signs Spending Bill, Vowing to
   Battle Earmarks," http://www.washingtonpost.com/wp-dyn/content/
   article/2009/03/11/AR2009031101499.html, March 12, 2009.
9. Scott Glabe, "Old Don Young Had a Farm: An accomplished porker
   tries to buy himself the chairmanship of the House Homeland Security
   Committee," http://www.weeklystandard.com/Content/Public/Articles/000/
   000/006/079wqklw.asp, September 20, 2005.
10. Ibid.
11. Web site: http://councilfor.cagw.org/site/PageServer?pagename=reports_
    earmarks (accessed January 4, 2010).
12. Glabe, "Old Don Young Had a Farm: An accomplished porker tries to buy
    himself the chairmanship of the House Homeland Security Committee,"
    September 20, 2005.

CHAPTER 14 THE MEDIA: LOSING ITS WAY

1. Web site: http://www.loc.gov/exhibits/jefferson/jefffed.html (accessed January 4, 2010).
2. Web site: http://www.brainyquote.com/quotes/quotes/r/ronaldreag183750 .html (accessed January 4, 2010).

★ PART IV: CONSERVATIVE SOLUTIONS TO OTHER
NATIONAL CHALLENGES

CHAPTER 15 A HEALTHY AMERICA

1. Web site: http://www.brainyquote.com/quotes/quotes/t/thomasjeff164329 .html (accessed January 4, 2010).
2. Web site: http://www.brainyquote.com/quotes/quotes/t/thomasjeff118441 .html (accessed January 4, 2010).
3. Web site: http://www.cms.hhs.gov/NationalHealthExpendData/02_ NationalHealthAccountsHistorical.asp#TopOfPage (accessed January 4, 2010).
4. Ibid.
5. Web site: http://www.cms.hhs.gov/NationalHealthExpendData/downloads/ nhegdp08 (accessed January 4, 2010).
6. Web site: http://www.kff.org/insurance/h08_7828.cfm (accessed January 4, 2010).
7. Ibid.
8. Web site: http://www.census.gov/hhes/www/hlthins/hlthin08/fig06.pdf (accessed January 4, 2010).
9. Web site: http://www.census.gov/hhes/www/hlthins/hlthin08/fig07.pdf (accessed January 4, 2010).
10. Web site: http://www.msnbc.msn.com/id/34448741 (accessed January 4, 2010).
11. Web site: http://www.cms.hhs.gov/apps/media/press/release. asp?Counter=2935 (accessed January 4, 2010).
12. Web site: http://www.cbo.gov/ftpdocs/87xx/doc8758/MainText.3.1.shtml (accessed January 4, 2010).
13. Web site: http://www.cdc.gov/pdf/facts_about_obesity_in_the_united_ states.pdf (accessed January 4, 2010).
14. Ibid.
15. Ibid.
16. Nanci Hellmich, "Rising obesity will cost U.S. health care $344 billion a year," http://www.usatoday.com/news/health/weightloss/2009-11-17-future -obesity-costs_N.htm, November 17, 2009.

17. Web site: http://care.diabetesjournals.org/content/32/suppl_2/S194.extract (accessed January 4, 2010).
18. Web site: http://www.newsweek.com/id/130621 (accessed January 4, 2010).
19. Web site: http://www.alz.org/national/documents/report_alzfactsfigures2009.pdf (accessed January 4, 2010).
20. Ibid.
21. "A Healthier America: 10 Top Priorities for Prevention," *Promoting Disease Prevention*, March 2008.
22. Web site: http://www.articlesbase.com/wellness-articles/cosmetic-surgery-statistics-rising-consumer-interest-377977.html (accessed January 4, 2010).

CHAPTER 16 ENTITLEMENT REFORM

1. From a fictionalized account of Cicero's *Life in a Pillar of Iron*, by Taylor Caldwell's *A Pillar of Iron* (New York: DoubleDay, 1965).
2. Web site: http://www.socialsecurity.gov/OACT/TRSUM/index.html (accessed January 4, 2010).
3. Web site: http://www.gpoaccess.gov/usbudget/fy10/pdf/budget/summary.pdf (accessed January 4, 2010).
4. Web site: http://www.ssa.gov/OACT/TRSUM/index.html (accessed January 4, 2010).
5. Ibid.
6. William G. Shipman, "Paulson's possible prosperity," http://washingtontimes.com/news/2006/jun/21/20060621-085639-9193r//, June 21, 2006.
7. Neil Howe and Richard Jackson, *2001 Chartbook on Entitlements and the Aging of America* (Alexandria VA: 2001).
8. Web site: http://www.ssa.gov/OACT/TRSUM/index.html (accessed January 4, 2010).
9. Ibid.
10. Ibid.
11. Social Security Trustees Report, April 2007 (intermediate projections)
12. Web site: http://www.ssa.gov/OACT/TRSUM/index.html accessed January 4, 2010).
13. Web site: http://www.ssa.gov/OACT/TRSUM/index.html (accessed January 4, 2010).
14. Ibid.
15. Ibid.

16. Jeffrey H. Anderson, "Annual Medicare Fraud: $60 Billion; Annual Profits of Top Ten Insurance Companies: $8 billion," http://www.weeklystandard .com/weblogs/TWSFP/2009/10/post_145.asp, October 31, 2009.

17. Carrie Johnson, "Medical Fraud a Growing Problem: Medicare Pays Most Claims Without Review," http://www.washingtonpost.com/wp-dyn/content/article/2008/06/12/AR2008061203915.html, June 13, 2008.

18. Web site: http://oig.hhs.gov/oei/reports/oei-09-07-00030.pdf (accessed January 4, 2010).

19. Ibid.

20. Web site: http://www.msnbc.msn.com/id/22184921/ (accessed January 4, 2010).

21. Ibid.

22. Jay Weaver, "Medicare agency stymied in quest for 'a pound of cure': The federal Medicare agency spends less than two-tenths of a cent of every dollar in its budget to fight abuse, waste and fraud." http://www .miamiherald.com/living/health/story/636745.html, August 11, 2008.

CHAPTER 17 REPOWERING THE UNITED STATES: THE ENERGY CHALLENGE

1. Web site: http://my.huckpac.com/?Fuseaction=TeamHuck.View&State_id=68 (accessed January 4, 2010).

2. Web site: http://tonto.eia.doe.gov/energyexplained/index.cfm?page=oil_where (accessed January 4, 2010).

3. Madlen Read, "Oil sets new trading record above $147 a barrel," http://www.usatoday.com/money/economy/2008-07-11-3815204975_x.htm, July 11, 2008.

4. Web site: http://tonto.eia.doe.gov/energyexplained/index.cfm?page=us_energy_home (accessed January 4, 2010).

5. Ibid.

6. Web site: http://tonto.eia.doe.gov/energyexplained/index.cfm?page=oil_home#tab2 (accessed January 4, 2010).

7. Ibid.

8. Ibid.

9. Ibid.

10. Ibid.

11. Web site: http://tonto.eia.doe.gov/dnav/pet/pet_move_impcus_a2_nus_ep00_im0_mbblpd_a.htm (accessed January 4, 2010).

12. Web site: http://pubs.usgs.gov/fs/fs-0028-01/fs-0028-01.pdf (accessed January 4, 2010).

13. Web site: http://www.heritage.org/Research/EnergyandEnvironment/ bg2341.cfm (accessed January 4, 2010).
14. Web site: http://tonto.eia.doe.gov/dnav/pet/pet_crd_crpdn_adc_mbblpd_ a.htm (accessed January 4, 2010).
15. Web site: http://www.eia.doe.gov/oiaf/aeo/excel/figure3over_data.xls (accessed January 4, 2010).
16. Web site: http://tonto.eia.doe.gov/energyexplained/index.cfm?page =natural_gas_home#tab2 (accessed January 4, 2010).
17. Web site: http://tonto.eia.doe.gov/energyexplained/index.cfm?page=coal_ reserves (accessed January 4, 2010).
18. Web site: http://tonto.eia.doe.gov/energyexplained/index.cfm?page=coal_ imports (accessed January 4, 2010).
19. Web site: http://www.fossil.energy.gov/programs/powersystems/ pollutioncontrols/overview_mercurycontrols.html (accessed January 4, 2010).
20. Web site: http://tonto.eia.doe.gov/energyexplained/index.cfm?page =renewable_home (accessed January 4, 2010).
21. Web site: http://tonto.eia.doe.gov/energyexplained/index.cfm?page =renewable_home (accessed January 4, 2010).
22. Web site: http://tonto.eia.doe.gov/energyexplained/index.cfm?page=wind_ electricity_generation (accessed January 4, 2010).
23. Web site: http://www1.eere.energy.gov/windandhydro/about.html (accessed January 4, 2010).
24. Web site: http://apps1.eere.energy.gov/news/daily.cfm/hp_news_id=41 (accessed January 4, 2010).
25. Web site: http://tonto.eia.doe.gov/energyexplained/index.cfm?page =nuclear_home#tab2 (accessed January 4, 2010).
26. Web site: http://www.world-nuclear.org/info/inf41.html (accessed January 4, 2010).
27. John Carey, "Nuclear's Tangled Economics: John McCain says new plants can help solve the energy crisis and address climate change. It's not that simple," http://www.businessweek.com/magazine/content/08_27/ b4091024354027.htm?chan=top+news_green+business+news+index+page_ policies, June 26, 2008.
28. Sharon Terlep, "GM Hopes Volt Juices Its Future," http://online.wsj.com/ article/SB124998537270122333.html, August 12, 2009.

CHAPTER 18 ENVIRONMENTAL ETHICS AND CONSERVATIVE VALUES

1. Web site: http://www.famousquotesandauthors.com/authors/thomas_ huxley_quotes.html (accessed January 4, 2010).

CHAPTER 19 ENDING ILLEGAL IMMIGRATION

1. Web site: http://www.famousquotesandauthors.com/authors/thomas_jefferson_quotes.html (accessed January 4, 2010).
2. Web site: http://www.cis.org/CurrentNumbers (accessed January 4, 2010).
3. Thomas Frank, "Illegal immigrant population declines," http://www.usatoday.com/news/nation/2009-02-23-immigration_N.htm, February 24, 2009.
4. Ibid.
5. Web site: http://www.cis.org/articles/2007/back1007.html (accessed January 4, 2010).
6. Web site: http://www.fairus.org/site/News2?page=NewsArticle&id=16723 (accessed January 4, 2010).
7. Web site: http://www.examiner.com/a-1321600-Use_money_transfers_to_stop_illegal_immigrants.html (accessed January 4, 2010).
8. Mark Landsbaum, "Amnesty By Any Other Name," http://97.74.65.51/readArticle.aspx?ARTID=8203, June 21, 2005 (accessed January 4, 2010).
9. Spencer S. Hsu and Kari Lydersen, "Illegal Hiring Is Rarely Penalized: Politics, 9/11 Cited in Lax Enforcement," http://www.washingtonpost.com/wp-dyn/content/article/2006/06/18/AR2006061800613.html, June 19, 2006.

CONCLUSION

1. Web site: http://www.theodoreroosevelt.org/life/quotes.htm (accessed January 4, 2010).
2. Web site: http://www.brainyquote.com/quotes/quotes/r/ronaldreag183976.html (accessed January 4, 2010).

ABOUT THE AUTHOR

TODD LONG WAS born in Arlington, Virginia, in 1964. He holds a BA in Economics from Rollins College and earned his law degree from Wake Forest University. He is a board-certified trial lawyer and has practiced in Orlando, Florida, for the past 20 years. After running for Congress in the 2008 Republican primary, and hosting his conservative talk-radio show, Todd has entered the 2010 Republican U.S. House race in Florida's Eight District. Todd and his wife, Ninette, are the proud parents of Noah (7) and Natalia (5).

Contact the Author

2423 Norfolk Rd.

Orlando, FL 32803

email: tlong3@cfl.rr.com